Barn Stalls, Rock Walls
& House Calls

Barn Stalls, Rock Walls & House Calls

A Country Veterinarian's Wit & Wisdom

Martin O. Kaplan, V. M. D

Animal Rescue League of Southern Rhode Island

South Kingstown, RI

To Dr. Martin Kaplan
We offer our heartfelt appreciation for the
gift of these stories from your incredible
life as a country veterinarian. For all of
the animals you have helped these many
years, and for those who cannot speak for
themselves, we thank you.

 The Animal Rescue League
of Southern Rhode Island

On the cover: Doctor Kaplan visits Casey Farm in Saunderstown,
Rhode Island, a working farm and a property of Historic New England.
(Photograph by Christopher Izzo, CRI Design, Cranston, RI)

First Edition November 2008
10 9 8 7 6 5 4 3 2 1

At my age, I feel so fortunate to have been surrounded by a close and loving family. My wife Evalyn persisted in encouraging me to tell my stories for others to enjoy, and I am sorry that she didn't live long enough to see this book. I am in constant touch with my brothers Arnold and Morey and their families in Pennsylvania. My son John insists on the movie rights. My niece Ann checks in daily and we dine weekly. Thank you, all. You mean so much to me.

M.O.K.

Contents

Foreword

I was there for many of the events that Doc recounts here, and, for those I did not witness, I have heard them many times, told by the master storyteller himself. No matter how many times Doc has told me his stories, I still enjoy hearing them over and over (and over) again. My one regret is that some of my favorite stories, the "juicy" ones, may be omitted in order to "protect the innocent."

I lost my biological father when I was a young boy. I loved and respected him deeply and no one could ever take his place. If anyone could come close, however, that person would be Doc Kaplan. Due to my father's untimely death, I lost the opportunity to have him as an integral part of my teenage and adult life. As a result, I had a longer relationship with Doc than my Dad. In some ways I think I developed a closer relationship with Doc Kaplan than I ever had with my father. Since my Dad's passing, Doc has been a father figure to me, one I could also talk with as a peer.

In many respects, Doc was not only like a father to me but also my best friend. I liken my relationship with him to the old judge in the Andy Hardy movies my parents enjoyed in the 1930s. The stories usually revolved around Andy, an ambitious, overzealous, girl-crazy youth who schemed himself into all kinds of trouble. He always ended up turning to his father, Judge Hardy, who never punished Andy or used his influence to get Andy out of trouble, but rather counseled him to do the right thing, whatever the consequences. Doc is the complete picture for me: a father, brother, best friend, confidant, mentor, and Judge Hardy. I'll always love him for what he has done for me and many other students who aspired to be veterinarians.

Although we wished to be like him, we all knew there could be only one Doc Kaplan.

Some of my favorite times were Saturdays in South County, Rhode Island. This was the day of the week when Doc took a group (mostly University of Rhode Island students) with him on farm calls. We would assist him, and he would teach us the correct way to restrain a horse for castration, treat a cow for milk fever, deliver a breech calf alive, replace a prolapsed uterus in an old cow, or determine the cause of a valuable show horse's lameness. Not only did he teach us veterinary medicine, he also engaged us in heated debates about current events. By the end of the day, we felt we had solved the world's problems.

I am very proud of those days. As we traveled over the scenic South County roads, I almost always got to sit in the front seat next to Doc. To the accompanying group of students, sitting up front was a great honor. It also meant that when we arrived at a farm, I had to get out to open and close the gates going across the dirt path leading to the barn.

I was very excited when Doc took me to see the great Seattle Slew win the second leg of the Triple Crown at Pimlico in 1977. Doc was offered a seat in the box of the famous trainer, John Lenzini, which he declined in favor of sitting in the stands with all the other spectators. We each bet two dollars on that powerful equine athlete and kept the winning tickets as souvenirs rather than cashing them in. My mother still has my ticket proudly displayed in her home.

Doc admires and respects all minorities and has a special affinity for the people of the Narragansett Tribe in South County. In Doc's own words, "I've been privileged in knowing the chief medicine man of the Narragansett Indian tribe here. One day when I was treating a cow for him, we talked about traditional Indian medicine. I couldn't believe some of the remedies that they handed down over time. They had a remedy for everything, and many of these remedies have evolved into modern-day medicine. From this I learned that there is a lot to be said for the Narragansetts, their culture, and how they take care of their people. They had a great deal of dignity and still do. I certainly respect their ways."

Another example of Doc's caring for all people—one evening, a group of boys, mostly African American and Native American and ranging in age from nine to twelve years, walked all the way to Doc's home office from Peace Dale, pulling a rusty old red wagon carrying their dog, a purebred American mutt that had been hit by a car. The dog was all banged up with contusions and lacerations over a good portion of his chest and abdomen. Doc had the kids wait outside for about an hour while he sutured and bandaged the wounds and administered antibiotics and pain medication. He then gently placed the dog back in the wagon. As the boys reached the bottom of Doc's driveway, one of them ran back and said, "Doc, I almost forgot, how much do I owe you?"

"How much do you have?"

"All together we have two dollars and forty-five cents."

Doc smiled and said, "That's exactly the right amount. How'd you know it was going to be two dollars and forty-five cents?"

With a big smile, the boy answered, "That's 'cause I figured what it would be worth."

Doc didn't take the money, the boys went home, and that tough-looking dog with the sad eyes made a great recovery and, I hope, stayed off the streets from then on.

As you read this marvelous book, just remember a few things that Doc taught me: the worth of a thing is what it will bring, cash is king; the best thing for a racehorse with a bowed tendon is a new owner; and breed the best to the best to get the best.

MICHAEL BRUZZI, D.M.V.

Preface

I talked forever about writing this book. My wife would laugh at all my stories and encourage me to record them, but, being a world-class procrastinator, I would just put it off and put it off.

What really inspired me was this. After I retired, if you could call it that, a farmer telephoned. "Doc, I hate to ask you, and I don't know whether you're still doing this kind of thing, but I've got a big Hereford cow here that's been trying to calve all night. The boy and I have tried to deliver it, but it's beyond us. We can't move it, and I wonder if you could come over and just give us some advice. I'd hate to lose this cow."

"Well, I'll see what I can do," I said. When I got to the farm, the cow was down in the field and had obviously been straining for quite a while. I put my arm in the cow and knew that the calf was not positioned properly. Unless I straightened it out, we would lose the calf and the mother. Well, after fifty years of using various techniques for manipulating deliveries, I repositioned the unborn calf in pretty short order and pulled it out. There were congratulations all around and I got in the car to head home.

By that time, it was dark and the moon was full. As I left the farm, I turned on a cassette tape that I had been playing nonstop. The Three Tenors, Carreras, Domingo, and Pavarotti, were in concert at the Los Angeles Coliseum before the soccer matches. I had those three brilliant tenors singing, the moon was shining, and I was on my way home. I was seventy-eight years old and still able to do the job. I felt really great about it. Along the way—it was about a forty-minute ride—I thought, "I really should write that book because this is a bygone era. It is a vanishing scene all over the country. It's just something I ought to do."

I had enjoyed all the Herriot books; our experiences were so similar. (At the time, I liked to joke with people who asked me if I was still practicing. I would tell them that I had cut back to twelve hours a day as a concession to my advancing years.)

There would be distractions at home, so we reserved a spot at Hilton Head, South Carolina, for a couple of weeks, for me to be free to work on the book. I was already familiar with the use of a tape recorder, having corresponded with a former veterinary student, Mike Bruzzi, when he was studying in Italy. I turned on the machine and filled up four tapes, both sides. On returning to Rhode Island, I found two people, Judy Phillips and Angela Weidinger—both animal lovers, owners of horse farms, and valued clients—to transcribe the tapes, a herculean task that produced more than 200 pages of double-spaced text. I distributed some copies to my family and close friends and considered the project finished.

A dozen years passed. In November 2007, soon after my 90th birthday, Bob Smith dropped by, finding me behind the house, cleaning out leaves in the swimming pool, preparing for winter. "Doc," said Bob, "have you done anything with that stack of paper you asked me to read? Diane was sorting out things the other day and came upon it. She thinks you should get it published." (Diane herself had published two collections of Rhode Island stories, *Rembrances of Life in Peace Dale and Wakefield*, and *The Hamlet of Perryville*.)

This started me thinking. At first, I couldn't imagine many people, other than family, who would be interested in my stories, but the Smiths persuaded me otherwise. That was when I decided to explore publishing them. I would underwrite the cost of production and printing, so any proceeds could go to the Animal Rescue League of Southern Rhode Island, the organization that was continuing the good work of Mrs. Avis Quigley, a friend to me when I was first stationed here in Rhode Island. The Smiths were acquainted with Mary Keane through the Pettaquamscutt Historical Society. Mary had retired from a career in publishing with the idea that she would help people tell their life stories, and after she read my manuscript she could not contain herself. Her enthusiasm was contagious. She ran my idea by the people at the Rescue League, and it didn't take long before they agreed to be involved. Then, Mary began to line up a team of talented local people to help with the book's production.

As I write this, it is Valentine's Day 2008, twelve years later, and at the urging of so many friends and former clients, I am finishing this book with the aid of many people. I still look forward to every day. I read three daily newspapers. I get half a dozen journals on small animal medicine and large animal medicine and exotic animal medicine and zoo animal medicine. I'm certainly fortunate that I still have all my senses. I have a great memory for things that happened in the past. I walk along the shore every day, missing only when the ocean is too rough, or if snow and ice cover the sidewalks. I watch TV, mostly world news and financial news.

And I have a loving family and so many friends. As far as retirement, I feel as if I'm not really retired, because I still have the interest and curiosity. Not a week goes by when I don't meet someone in town who asks me about a horse problem or a cow problem. In fact, I ran into Casey Conrad at the grocery store the other day, which reminded me to include one more story which involves her father, Dr. Bob Conrad, the first surgeon on staff at the South County Hospital (see "Spud Mac's Steer").

This project has reawakened old ties and made some new ones for me. I have so many people to thank for their continuing support and friendship. Bob and Diane Smith go all the way back to the time I first lived here—they remember it when. Diane's father was the herdsman at the University of Rhode Island dairy barn for some years, and also at various other Rhode Island farms (including Kirkbrae Farm in Lincoln). Years ago, I took care of the horse that Ibby Freeman boarded at Casey Farm, and I was delighted to find out that Ibby has been active in the Rescue League all these years.

Above: At Casey Farm, Ibby
Freeman and Katie Grimes
head eastward. (Photo
courtesy of Elizabeth and
Archie MacLaughlin)

Right: Ibby Freeman seated on
Hutch at Casey Farm

It turns out that young Casey Conrad is quite the entrepreneur and is giving her talents in many ways to market and distribute this book. Pat and Ted Kostarides sustain me still.

I hope you enjoy my stories.

MARTIN O. KAPLAN, V.M.D

Assignment in Kingston

1945. That was the year I arrived in Kingston, Rhode Island, a fairy-story college town in South County (officially, Washington County). It was surrounded by farms and boasted the finest dairy herds in the country. There was a milking parlor where you could watch the cows being milked and order ice cream and purchase rich pasteurized milk, homemade butter, and eggs.

Having completed my education and served as an officer in the Army's Veterinary Corps, I accepted a position with the Federal Bureau of Animal Industry to test cattle for tuberculosis and for brucellosis (undulant fever in humans). At first I was assigned to New Hampshire, then to Boston, and finally to Kingston, based at Rhode Island State College, now the University of Rhode Island.

I rented a large front bedroom in the home of the former college president Howard Edwards on North Road. I took my evening meals with various faculty members at the Lambda Chi fraternity house. The meals were excellent and a weekly meal ticket was reasonable. I was able to attend plays, listen to nationally known speakers, and had contact with people from the various departments at the college.

And when I got home at night, there would be a letter waiting for me from my girlfriend, Evalyn Daniels, soon to become my wife. At the time, she was secretary to the dean of the dental school at the University of Pennsylvania, where we had met. She never missed a day, and I would write back to her about the events of my day, and look forward to her visits and our getting married as soon as we were able.

The job that I had at the time was considered a good one. I

1

made $55 a week and got paid every two weeks. Once Evalyn and I were married, we rented an apartment in Kingston right next to the college. Two bedrooms, bath, nice kitchen, and all utilities included for $50 a month.

The government job had some advantages. I was given a Bureau of Animal Industry car. I needed to work only about twenty hours a week and received a princely salary. In addition, I had sick leave, holidays, and a retirement plan that would enable me to quit after twenty years. Every few years, if I stayed out of trouble, I would be promoted with a pay increase. We had great hopes that we could save at least half my salary toward our dream of owning a farm. That was the beginning. But it didn't take long for me to realize that all my years of education were being wasted doing a simple job that I could teach a technician to do in a month.

After high school, I had attended a three-year agricultural school, the National Farm School in Doylestown, Pennsylvania, known today as Delaware Valley College. The school was a 2,000-acre farm that offered dairy husbandry, poultry husbandry, agronomy, floriculture, horticulture, forestry, and crops. Tractors at that time were not generally available, so most of the work we did was with teams of horses. We were self sufficient, actually living on what we produced on the farm. I received an excellent agricultural education.

I was a fairly good athlete and played football, baseball, basketball, and especially enjoyed boxing. I won a scholarship to Penn State for football and boxing. After three years, I was accepted at the University of Pennsylvania and spent the next four years getting my veterinary degree. Things haven't changed that much in the intervening years; the education we received was equivalent to any medical education. In fact, in the first year, we competed with and took classes with the medical school students.

While I was testing the cattle, I discovered that most of the land in South County was agrarian and people made their living by farming. As I got to know the dairy farmers, they would tell me about their difficulty in getting veterinarians to come here and practice, which certainly was my goal.

There was very little veterinary service here, even for small animals. In 1938, with a little support from the town, Avis Quigley and some dedicated volunteers had opened a small shelter for abandoned or abused animals. They had a no-kill policy, which meant that the animals accumulated. When I met Mrs. Quigley, I was still working for the federal government but I would volunteer to take care of the shelter animals when I could. This shelter was really the beginning of the present Animal Rescue League of Southern Rhode Island, which has expanded and now serves a good part of the county.

Federal, State, and Private Practice

I began work in Rhode Island as a federal veterinarian. Normally, federal veterinarians would be assigned to test cattle for brucellosis and tuberculosis. During World War II many of our professionals were called away into the armed services, so cattle testing was being managed by the state veterinarian, who divided the spoils among a few Rhode Island veterinarians. After the war, I came along.

Being a federal veterinarian, I didn't have much contact with the state veterinarian; I would meet in Providence with my federal overseers from Boston. I was independent, but I quickly found out that the state was a closed corporation. The few veterinarians who were here had pretty well divided the state into territories. They managed to keep exclusive by not allowing newcomers in. In order to be certified as a practicing veterinarian, you had to take a state examination. Since this small group gave the examinations, it was said that most of the questions were rigged—you never heard of what they were asking for, things like old compounds and old medications. I was told right from the beginning about this. After I had been here a little over a year, the state veterinarians began asking me if I was going to go into practice. They were worried about whether I posed any threat to them and their state assignments.

A prominent lawyer in town, Ira Lloyd Letts, was a man with a social conscience who didn't tolerate a lot of the things that went on. When Judge Letts asked me about my going into private practice, I told him that it was very difficult to get a license in Rhode

Island, but I was planning to take the State Boards. He told me, "You take the State Boards, and if you have any problems, I'd be glad to help you out." I passed the examination, which meant, of course, that I could go into practice. When I began, I lived in Kingston, not far from one of the members of the State Board, and, from the feedback I got, he wasn't very happy.

Judge Letts lived just about five miles north of me and maintained a beautiful herd of Aberdeen Angus cattle. It had been a long time since his cattle had been tested, so he asked me to call at his barn. Aberdeen Angus cattle are not domesticated. They're very wild and hard to handle; you had to start by getting their heads into chutes to immobilize them. Only then could you draw the blood and use the tuberculin to test them for tuberculosis. I told him that I would have to have a chute and that we'd need people there to help me.

He made the arrangements, and I went there on a Sunday. For the next two hours we proceeded to lasso the cattle, get them in the chutes, and get them all tested. When I had finished, Judge Letts asked me to come to the house. He went into another room and came back with a very expensive bottle of whiskey and a couple of boxes of Haddon Hall cigars. I didn't smoke or drink, but he wanted to show his gratitude, even though I protested that I was doing this as part of my government job. He then put a fifty-dollar bill on top of the box of cigars and said, "Thank you very much, Dr. Kaplan." So I took the cigars and the whiskey and the fifty-dollar bill (I had never seen a fifty-dollar bill.) When I got home, my wife was waiting for me. "Look what I got," I said. Needless to say, we went out and celebrated; I had a big steak and we had money left over.

Once I had my license and was becoming well known, I ran into a problem. Theodore Francis Greene, the senior U.S. Senator from Rhode Island, had decided that a proposed foot-and-mouth disease research laboratory would be a great boondoggle for the state. He had enough seniority so that, when it came to pork-barrel spending, he could demand this kind of thing, which went on then just as much as it does today. Greene suggested that Prudence Island, a little island in the middle of Narragansett Bay, not far from the mainland, would be a perfect place to put this multi-million dollar laboratory.

Of course, all the politicians jumped on the bandwagon to support the laboratory, and all my farmer friends formed an organization to oppose it. The farmers asked me to be their spokesperson. It led to discussions, with the farmers on one side and the politicians on the other. One of the state veterinarians, a political insider, called a meeting of veterinarians to support the laboratory on Prudence Island.

I went to the meeting. There were a dozen or more veterinarians all ready to support the politicians. One of them stood up and said, "I'd like a unanimous resolution from this society. All those in favor, say aye." They all said aye, but I said nay. He acted as if he hadn't heard me. So, I stood up and said, "Wait a minute. I just voted against the resolution, so it's not unanimous. You know how I feel. You've seen enough of the articles and been at the preliminary meetings." I won't name the man. He's since died, and I wouldn't want to hurt any of his family's feelings, but he then stood up and said, "I move that we vote to kick Dr. Kaplan out of this society, and that way it'll be unanimous." And he won that resolution.

I immediately called Judge Letts, whose reaction was, "They what? You let me take care of this." He made some calls to the state veterinarian and the governor and others. He told them that he would oppose this in court, and that he would likely file suit against these people. He had plenty of grounds, he said, for damages. He put the fear of God into them; they weren't eager to engage any further.

Before we finished, we had experts from all over who came to Rhode Island and testified how rats, wild animals, and seagulls could very easily pick up this live virus from the island and drop it onto their cattle herds. That killed the Prudence Island resolution. That laboratory is now located on Plum Island, off the northeast coast of Long Island, New York.

The Way We Work

Beginning with my generation, we had a Board of Examiners here in Rhode Island, and I was fortunate to be appointed by three different governors—Notte, Garrahy, and Chafee—and therefore had a role in how the national exams came to be. Today, everybody takes the same examination, countrywide. As things evolved, of course, the profession changed. Women arrived at parity with the men and have become leaders in all the professions. (In fact, seventy percent of veterinary students today are women, and the schools are giving extra points to men who apply—a case of affirmative action in reverse!)

Also, today, doctors, dentists, and veterinarians schedule a lot of time off. They work only four or five days a week; they have their weekends and their evenings. They have to have time with their families. If that's the way they want to practice today, that's fine, I suppose.

The veterinary journals are constantly taking surveys, telling people how to increase their income; there are specialists who give seminars on the subject. The professional meetings I go to are jammed with people who want to know how to maximize their practices and make more money. The American Veterinary Medical Association did an extensive survey on the economics of veterinary medicine. After much money and expert input, the conclusion was that the people who work the most hours make the most money! Now, that sounds like a joke, but to me, that's exactly where it's at.

I have always believed in taking a couple of vacations a year, and I also attend professional meetings. I have been all over the world. You might ask, "Since you worked by yourself, what happened to your clients when you were away?" Well, I always made arrangements with veterinarians in this area; they agreed to cover for me, and I would cover for them in the same way. We've never been afraid of losing clients that way. It was understood that we didn't accept those people as regular clients. Our system worked very well. In certain parts of the country, groups of veterinarians agree to cover each other one weekend a month so that their clients have somebody that they can go to in an emergency.

The way I always wanted to practice, and did, was to live and work in the same place so that I could be available to my clients twenty-four hours a day. My young friend, Dr. Bruzzi, has the same attitude. In his first years of practice, he was devoted to his practice and quickly prospered. He was totally involved. But that seems to be a bygone era and nobody thinks that way anymore. I'm sad because of it.

A Typical Day

[This story, by Bill Rodriguez, appeared in *The Narragansett Times - Standard-Times*, South County Edition on January 2, 1986, and is reprinted here with permission.]

Witness to four decades' change
Doc Kaplan, roaming veterinarian

A certain rhythm to your day comes about when you've worked with animals all your life.

Take farm chores. Regardless of the international political situation, cows have to be milked. No matter whether you're a young boy in the throes of puppy love or a grey-haired gentleman well into his pension years, the horses must be fed. So wars may come and life crises may go, but the steady pulse of those daily chores marks the pace of people such as Doc Kaplan.

Martin O. Kaplan, V.M.D., has entered his 40th year as a farm veterinarian. For most of those years he has been in private practice, traveling all over southern

9

Rhode Island to attend to a 1 a.m. calf birthing or milk fever crisis here, a spavined horse hock there.

And every morning his day begins the same. Now that there are so few calls to make, what with the decline in farms and horse stables, he no longer gets up at 5 a.m. Nowadays it's 7:30 when he steps outside onto the 40 acres he and his wife have on Tower Hill Road, just before the first Wakefield exit when you're heading south on Route 1. Evalyn is also his invaluable one-person office staff, doing everything from bookkeeping to assisting with treatments in the clinic.

The frosted grass stubble crunched underfoot as Kaplan trudged the 100 yards across the roadside pasture, heading toward the stables. The grass stood rooted in a slight furrow that lay in a beeline between the single storey house on the hill and the gate he was heading toward. A plaid golf cap covered a balding head and a fringe of grey hair clipped to military shortness. Not a New Englander by birthright, he has become a kind of Swamp Yankee by osmosis over the years: A sincere friendliness taking the edge off of a blunt, no-nonsense manner.

The air was a bit nippy, so he wore a tan parka with a wool lining, and his hands were protected by thick leather gloves. Over the decades there has been many a time that he made this trek through snow up to his belly.

At the barn area, he sprinkled a few handfuls of kibble onto the cement floor of a shed. Numerous cats and several chipmunk-sized kittens flocked his way; some nearly feral ones threw themselves into reverse when they noticed a stranger with him. They all have the same name, "kitty," he remarked with a smile as he called to them.

Outside the door he gestured to an aluminum ladder leading to a hay loft, as one skittish cat clambered up it as quickly as a fox up a log.

Kaplan unbolted one of the stalls and let out Pip, his black Labrador and walking companion, pausing to give him a few reassuring pats. Then he filled a bucket with a rich mixture of corn, oats, and bran sweetened with molasses, plus a portion of top-grade Canadian white oats. He brought breakfast over to another stall, which housed his current pride and joy, as yet unnamed.

"This yearling filly is fourth generation for me since I've been raising horses," he said, keeping his eyes on the bay's graceful lines as he stroked her. "She is a beautiful animal. That's what I've been breeding for."

The Thoroughbred filly was born last spring in Maryland.

"Being born in Rhode Island is useless, because there are no special programs for Rhode Island breeds," he explained. "If you are Maryland bred there are $6 million in extra bonuses, purses, for all the races in Maryland."

Kaplan stepped over to say good morning to Scherzo's Last, the filly's mother, a few stalls away. As a stakes winner, this race horse has brought him over $100,000 in winnings over the years. He led her to a nearby paddock and watched as she galloped off for her morning exercise.

The grunt work of farm life was about to begin. He got the hay pitchfork and began to toss the mare's manure and soiled bedding into a wheelbarrow, talking about the decline of Rhode Island farms as he worked.

When he settled in the state in 1945, testing cows for the U.S. government, dairy farms alone numbered, by his guess, something like 600 or 700. Back then, when farmers bottled, pasteurized and delivered their own milk, he could look up and down a side road in South County and count five or ten dairy farms.

"There were probably 6,000, 6,500 cows in Newport County alone," he said of an area where he did a lot of tuberculin testing. "Now there aren't 650 dairy cows in the whole state."

They built on the Wakefield land in 1954, eventually carving four wide pastures out of the 40 acres of woodland. Even then, when the center divider of what is now Route 1 was their front lawn, the area was decidedly rural. On an average day they would see perhaps a dozen cars go by, he said, while nowadays they can't get out of their driveway during the summer crush.

Quitting the cushy sinecure of a government job in 1950, Kaplan set out to be a country veterinarian, against the economic advice of the two other vets then in the area. But testing blood samples of dairy cows was not what the vigorous 33-year-old saw as his life's work. After all, he had more years of preparation behind him than most physicians.

Growing up on a Pennsylvania farm in the late 1930s, he first went to agricultural school on a football and baseball scholarship. To young vets today who complain about the rigors of their training, he is inclined to mention that these three years between high school and college involved spending 365 days per year on a working farm, except for one weekend per month to visit home.

A football and boxing scholarship got him to Penn State for three years of pre-vet studies, followed by four years at the University of Pennsylvania in veterinary medicine. Then there were two years in the Army—cavalry, of course—and work as a dairy inspector in New Hampshire, Boston, and finally the Kingston campus. Then called Rhode Island College, it had 600 students and the second largest ag school milking parlor in the East.

Quitting the secure job also meant putting 9 to 5 hours behind him forever.

"I worked 16, 18 hours a day. Almost every morning I was out of bed by 5. And midnight, 1, 2 o'clock in the morning was nothing unusual for me to be going on farm calls," he related, then added the most important part: "And really enjoying it."

When he started out there were ten vets in the state. Today there are more than 100. Over the years he has seen a lot of young animal lovers, aspiring veterinarians just setting up practice, smile at him as they picture themselves in his shoes. He's also watched that smile fade away.

"They start out saying they're going to do cows, they're going to be farm veterinarians, riding the highways and byways like old Herriot. Let me see that guy a year from now—where's he going to be? First of all, he's not going to like the shit we're going to be wallowing in, or the smell, or the inconvenience, or the economic suicide of making farm calls for a small fraction of what you can make with dogs and cats," Kaplan began, warming to the subject.

"You don't have to be an economist to figure out that if it takes you two hours to make one farm call and you get $25, and you can see 12 small animals in that time and get $25 each... You don't need anybody to do a business survey to tell you what you should be doing from the standpoint of money."

But as with James Herriot, the author of *All Creatures Great and Small*, the operative word in the expression "making a living" is the last one. As the number of farms declined, he gradually shifted his practice toward taking care of pets in the afternoons and evenings, but his heart is still in the countryside. Martin Kaplan says he would rather make a leisurely farm call, chat about sports, maybe be invited in for a cup of coffee, than play 18 holes of golf.

He gave an example from the other day. "Somebody apologized for calling me on Sunday. When I got there she apologized again, and I said: "Listen. Believe it or not, this is the biggest pleasure in the world. It's a beautiful day. I'm out in the country. I've finished my work at home."

After he trotted the battered blue wheelbarrow over to the steaming manure pile that towered higher than he stood, Doc Kaplan dumped the last of the soiled bedding and returned to freshen up his prize mare's stall. First he sprinkled lime around. Then he spread out a few flakes of leftover feed silage, sweet smelling clover hay and grass, shaking loose the compressed squares with the pitchfork. There would be no cheap wood chips here. Done, he paused a moment to survey the work, as one might after putting down fresh sheets in the guest room.

When he was done with his chores, he set off on that morning's schedule of rounds. His ritual began amidst the sizzles and breakfast smells of Phil's Restaurant, in downtown Wakefield, where he can be found at the counter every morning that it's open, around 8:30. On this particular morning he would be off to Casey's Farm in Saunderstown, to check on a sick goat he had been treating. Then he was to go to the Browning farm in Matunuck and the Kenyon farm in Richmond.

The first visit was just as leisurely as he had described his rounds to be. With Archie MacLaughlin towering over him in his overalls, in short order he checked the udder abscess on the goat, declared it to be closing up properly, and soon got down to purely socializing. Amidst ducks and geese scattering before them in the yard, MacLaughlin headed to a pasture and proudly showed off the herding prowess of a new Shepherd dog he had been training. Little black and white Kyle swung wide around the scattered herd and drove them to his master, who now and then uttered a brief command. Kaplan smiled and nodded his approval.

At that first farm he was accompanied by Michael Bruzzi, a 30-year-old Pawtucket native just about to take his certification boards after years of veterinary study in Italy. For the past 11 years he has been helped in various ways by Kaplan, as have several other young veterinarians now in practice. Eventually he will be sharing an expanded practice with Kaplan—who has no intentions of retiring.

"He was a legend then, when I was at URI," the 1977 graduate said of Kaplan. "He was the horse man."

The elderly vet had earlier spoken of never sending out bills but having "not one nickel" in bad debts to write off; of being proud that he has never refused to treat an animal because its owner didn't know when he'd be able to pay. How that all came about became clear after Bruzzi volunteered some information, something that he said was important to know about Doc Kaplan and the people he deals with. "They're not just there with their animals—they bring him their problems. A lot of people really love him for that," he declared. "I'd like to have that rapport when I become a vet."

Making a Living as a Veterinarian

In 1945 there was no industry around here. The town was mostly agrarian, and the main occupation was dairy farming. The farms were not large but they were very fertile, and the farmers were, almost without exception, Yankee stock. The family farms in most instances had been in the family for generations, and the children would continue as farmers and dairy farmers.

In the village of Wakefield, part of South Kingstown, we had no major chains or grocery stores: there was only one bank, one diner, one farm equipment store, one automobile agency, Albert Weibel's newspaper store on Main Street next to the Bell Block, and a mom-and-pop grocery store, called Stedmans, which was run by the Dexters, a family of dairy farmers.

In the summer, the population, particularly of Narragansett Pier next door, would swell with wealthy people from New York and Pennsylvania. They came with their polo ponies, their pets, and the help needed to staff their estates. The rest of the year I was totally occupied with taking care of large animals, and I gradually became the only veterinarian in the area who focused on cattle.

The local farmers really had no professional veterinary help, so I found myself being urged to quit my job with the government and go into private practice. The big debate with my wife was whether we could afford to give up the security of my government job with almost no money in the bank to start a practice. Could I make a living? The answer came from the manager of a large dairy farm called Horseshoe Falls in Shannock, nearby.

The farm had developed a national reputation for producing dairy cows that were big milk producers and had been winning at national shows for their conformation. (The farm was owned by an industrialist, George P. Clark, who had developed a method of

15

making narrow fabric, an elastic material, that changed the way underclothing would be designed. The product resulted in a great deal of wealth for the Clarks and enabled him to have a beautiful barn with very valuable Guernsey cattle.)

The manager of the Horseshoe Falls farm, Alfred "Ted" Browning, called me one Sunday and asked if I could help him out. One of his best cows had broken a horn and was bleeding profusely. All his attempts to stop the bleeding had failed, and they were unable to get a veterinarian. I told him that, while working for the government, I was not allowed to practice privately. I would come over and help him, but I wouldn't accept any payment. So, my wife and I drove over there and I took care of the cow. (The procedure involves cutting the remaining part of the horn close enough to the animal's head so that I could grab the artery inside and tie it off.) Afterwards, Ted said, "Well, if you won't accept any money, I'd like to take you to dinner." We thought that would be okay. Ethically, we didn't feel we could get into trouble with something like dinner.

Over dinner, we discussed the reasons why I could not seriously consider entering private practice. I explained that it was largely financial and that I was not about to give up a secure

Horseshoe Falls, Shannock

government job on a chance. He assured me that I would be successful. And furthermore, he asked, "How much are you making working for the government?" When I told him $220 a month, he said he would talk to Mr. Clark the next day to see if they could offer some kind of inducement to be the herd veterinarian, which meant that I would be on call whenever needed and also do the routine work.

The following day, Ted called me to say that Mr. Clark would be willing to guarantee me $400 a month as a retainer. That removed any objections that I might have had as far as the security of my going into practice and being able to make a living. With that, I notified the Bureau of Animal Industry in Boston that I was resigning.

An Emergency on Christmas Eve

Before going into practice for myself, when I was still working for the government, I received a call on Christmas Eve 1945 from Elmer Benson, a dairy farmer whose cows I had tested. "I'm sorry to call you on Christmas Eve, and I know this is an imposition, but my best cow is down, paralyzed, having just had a calf." Elmer thought it was milk fever.

Milk fever is an eclampsia, a condition seen quite frequently in cows after calving. The condition is caused by a lowering of blood calcium and the treatment is very simple: replacing the calcium results in a rapid, almost miraculous, recovery. A cow that is flat out, actually dying, paralyzed and unable to get up can be revived almost instantly with an infusion of calcium into the bloodstream. The problem was that I didn't have any drugs or equipment.

The only thing I could suggest to Elmer was an old trick, in fact the only remedy before the discovery of calcium replacement, which became the treatment of choice. It consisted of inserting what was called a "teat tube," or cannula, into the teat canal and attaching a bicycle pump to pump up the udder with air. If enough air is infused, you can stop the loss of calcium from the bloodstream. It's hard to explain, but it works.

Elmer said he had the teat tubes and a bicycle pump, but he didn't know how to infuse an udder, so I drove over there. The cow was flat on the barn floor, her ears were cold, and she was having difficulty breathing. A few more hours and she would have succumbed. We inserted the teat tubes, attached the bicycle pump, and started to pump up her udder. When the udder was full of air, we tied off all the teats to keep the air from escaping.

18

Then we propped up the cow so that she wouldn't choke and we made her comfortable, expecting results in ten or fifteen minutes. We went over to the house for a cup of coffee and some homemade cake. In the meantime, Elmer's son was in the barn watching the cow. In about fifteen minutes, he came rushing into the house, all excited, and said the cow was up and had walked into her stall. We all went to the barn and rejoiced at this successful outcome.

At that point, Elmer took out his wallet and said that he'd like to pay me for my trouble and that, it being Christmas Eve, he would pay me anything that I wanted.

"Elmer, I'm not allowed to take any money as long as I'm working for the government and I don't want to get into any trouble, so I'd rather you just consider this a favor."

"Well, I'm going to put twenty dollars in a jar on the top shelf of the cupboard, and the day you go into practice for yourself, I'm going to be your first client and that twenty dollars is going to be the first money that you make as a practicing veterinarian."

That was prophetic, because it wasn't long after that I accepted Ted Browning's offer to be the veterinarian for George P. Clark's farm, when I decided to go into practice for myself. It was a decision I've never regretted. I've had so many wonderful years of practice, and that was the beginning.

Opportunity Lost?

When I first started working in Rhode Island for the federal government, those who lived on Block Island were mainly fishermen or dairy farmers. There were about 300 cows on the island, and the milk was shipped by ferry to the mainland. It was my job to go to Block Island every year and spend an entire week there, blood testing cattle for tuberculosis and brucellosis according to federal regulations.

Mr. Dodge, from a Block Island family dating back to colonial days, was the principal dairy farmer on the island. When I was expected, he would meet me at the ferry and put me up at his house for the week. He would notify all the farmers on the island when I was on the way over. At night, his wife would prepare our meals and we would sit around, talking and listening to the radio. Mr. Dodge informed me at one of these evening sessions that he was thinking of retiring. He was going to move to the village, near the ferry landing, where he had a little cottage, and he wanted to sell his farm.

Today, Block Island still has permanent residents, but the population swells in the summer. Beautiful homes have been built; land is at a premium. If you owned ten acres of land on Block Island today, I'm sure you could sell it for a million dollars. In the late 1940s, land was cheap. Mr. Dodge informed me that his asking price was $35,000 for over one hundred acres of land, including forty to sixty milking cows, young stock, and machinery, equipment, the house, and the barn. He was willing to take ten percent down, and he offered to take the mortgage for the balance at four percent interest. That was a pretty exciting prospect. Mr. Dodge delivered me to the ferry at the end of the week and my wife met me.

When my wife asked how my week went, I said that it was great and that I had some news. I proceeded to tell her about this gorgeous farm surrounded by water and that I was thinking that it would be a great investment.

"You mean to tell me that you would spend that much money for a farm on Block Island when we haven't got our own farm or own place?"

"Well, it might take us a little longer."

That discussion did not last very long, because I was informed that we were not about to invest what we had saved on land in the middle of nowhere.

As it happened, the person who inherited that farm was not interested in selling or developing it. He turned it over to the Nature Conservancy, so the land is preserved forever. I can only imagine how we might have become multimillionaires. We jokingly talked about it for a long time after that.

How We Got Our Land

As soon as I decided to go into private practice, my wife and I placed an ad in the local paper announcing that I was available to provide veterinary care, and with that the phone started ringing.

Starting my practice in Kingston, we saved every penny we could, and it wasn't a year before we had $5,000, an accomplishment that we were very pleased about. I was working very hard. Twenty-four hours a day, seven days a week, and we were very careful. I bought used equipment and drove an old, beat-up car that I had paid fifty dollars for. Now that I had this bankroll, we started to look for land.

At that time, most of the good land in South Kingstown was owned by the Hazard family. T. P. Hazard was a wonderful man, very concerned about his town and the workers in his mills. The town still bears evidence of his family's philanthropy. The town hall, community center, libraries, and school sites all were gifts to the town from the Hazards. T. P. Hazard's sister was married to a landowner named Rush Sturges; they lived in the area where I live today called Tower Hill. It was just outside the town of Wakefield on a two-lane road, which is now a major highway, Route 1, but at that time it was country.

Hazard knew who I was because he had seen me at Mrs. Quigley's shelter; it was there that he had asked me when I was going to find a suitable place for him and others to bring their small animals for treatment. After I thought about it, I decided to stop in at Hazard's office in Peace Dale to tell him that I was looking for land but couldn't find any that was not owned by the Hazards. He asked me what I had in mind, and I told him that I understood that he had a big tract of land on Tower Hill, which would be a great place. He said, "Well, I do have some land up there, but how much money do you want to spend?" I told him I had $5,000 but didn't want to spend all of it on land. He said for $5,000 he couldn't help me but that he had some land across from his sister's farm. He didn't know how she'd feel about having a veterinarian across the road, but he said he'd talk to her about it.

He called me back and said his sister was agreeable, but I was not to keep any dogs that would entice her dogs to cross the road and possibly get hit by a car. I said that was fine with me. Then, he got his map out and showed me how much land he would sell for $3,500. He said there was about an acre of land there.

"Mr. Hazard, I want to buy a farm, I don't want to buy a house lot. I want to have a farm and an acre's not a farm."

"Well, you know, $3,500 is not a lot of money."

As it turned out, that was the Yankee way. Although T. P. Hazard was a wealthy man, he enjoyed dickering and bartering and that was the custom, so I said I'd wait. "Well, how much land did you have in mind?"asked he, and I pointed out a piece of land, about fifteen acres.

"No, no, no. $3,500 is not nearly enough."

"I have $5,000, but I need a little money left over so I can start my building in six months or a year."

After having a lot of fun with me, he agreed to sell me a beautiful piece of land that was partly cleared but exactly what I wanted: fifteen acres on top of a hill with a gorgeous view and excellent soil.

Then he said, "Now, you know, there's twenty-five acres of land behind that fifteen I'm willing to sell you, and the access to the road is right through the land you just bought. It would be wise if you bought that land too. It's got a stream on it and it's some beautiful land."

I had walked through this land. "I don't know, Mr. Hazard, how much do you want for those twenty-five acres?"

Without blinking an eye, he said, "I'd take $1,500 for it."

That meant he was going to get all my money. It was no accident that he offered it to me for the $1,500 he knew I still had.

I told him I'd have to go home and talk it over with my wife, which I did, and she said she'd leave it up to me. I went back later and told him, "Mr. Hazard, I'll give you $1,200, which will leave me just $300 in the bank." We went back and forth. He wanted $1,300, but finally I gave him $1,250 for the rest of the land.

Building a Home and a Farm

Now that we had our land, we needed to clear it in order to make a pasture. We arranged for people with bulldozers and moving equipment to move some of the rocks and brush. At that point, we had enough money to start building the house and foundation. We found the plans from a book I had bought at Weibel's news store: a Cape Cod house with my office at one end, where I could be available in the evenings to treat dogs and cats, diversifying my practice.

In the old days, it was not uncommon to have the office and house together and to be available twenty-four hours a day. It was a great way for me to work. I ended up having a very nice house built by a man who was known around here as Lightning Tefft. Lightning got that name because he was fast. He was a master builder. It was so natural for him. He wasn't formally educated, but he grew up building things. He took my plans and added some things that I wanted, and he started building.

We built the house and animal hospital before we had to borrow from the bank. Part of the agreement was that we could pay off the thirty-year mortgage early without penalty. We drove an old beat-up car and didn't eat out that often. My wife, a great saver, would lament, "We don't own the place, the bank does." She hated to owe money. So, a little more than three years later, we made the last payment.

My wife did everything. She kept the place clean. She answered the phone. She paid the bills. We lived and practiced here. We had a nice, little place here in the country, and it was paradise.

After we completed the house and office, I set about building the barns I needed from a set of plans I'd found in a magazine. I had become acquainted with many of the Narragansett Indians since I came here. They were master stonemasons. I would speculate that they learned their trade by building the beautiful stone fences that remain around South County. I hired some of these Narragansetts, from the Thomas and the Mars families, to build two beautiful barns of cement block and stone, with seven stalls—the animals could not kick down a stone structure, or chew on anything. Now I had my barns and twenty-five acres of cleared land all fenced with post-and-rail cedar cut out of the native swamps. I had everything I ever wanted and had an active, thriving animal practice. I was doing some small animal work in the afternoon, but my principal work was still with the dairy farmers.

Eventually I built a swimming pool in the back, a forty-by-twenty in-ground pool with a heater, and the neighbors and

The Kaplan barns (photo courtesy of Martha Watson Pena)

children's playmates would come over and enjoy it. Many times, on a Wednesday, which was supposed to be my day off, somebody would come around back and find me in the pool, and say, "Hey, doctor, I hope I'm not bothering you, but I got a sick cat that's . . . ." and I'd go to the office.

Dander

At this point, now that I had my barns, I decided to acquire a racehorse. B. A. Dario, a client, had built a couple of racetracks for Thoroughbreds and had started a breeding operation. He had an orphan foal whose mother had died birthing. Dario had too many other horses to bother with this orphan, so he offered to give him to me. We took him home, using a mother goat to nurse him, and we raised him.

He was my first horse. His father was a stallion named Bull Dandy, by a famous racehorse named Bull Lea (those bloodlines would be familiar to Thoroughbred horse people). We named him Dander after his father, and he turned out to be a good racehorse. We won quite a few races with him and then sold him. So, our first venture with Dander was a success—an encouraging way to begin training racehorses.

The Nubian Goat

After I had the horse barns, I acquired a baby Nubian goat, a green, undisciplined goat with long ears, a crooked face and a crooked nose, a very homely goat. This goat fell in love with me and from the time I got him, he wouldn't let me out of his sight. The only way I could get rid of him was to lock him in a stall.

We kept our stable meticulous; we swept up two or three times a day, so there wasn't even a piece of straw out there when we finished. The big problem with this goat was that it would follow me or anybody else who was sweeping, and he would drop his little pellets all over the place. We didn't think this was funny at all. We would shoo him away with the broom and try to discourage him, but he was not to be discouraged and he got to be a nuisance. If I went to get grain for the horses, he'd be in the grain room, standing on his hind legs, getting his face in the grain. If I set down a bucket with grain in it, he would knock it over. I was getting pretty frustrated with this goat.

Then, a man from Connecticut called and wanted me to look at a horse that was lame. He said, "It's a long way, but I have a good van, and if you could see him, I'd truck him up to your place." He drove up with his young son in a nice truck and trailer with the horse in back. When he went back to unload the horse, the son spotted the goat. The boy jumped out of the truck, ran over and threw his arms around the goat, and started hugging him and kissing him. Of course, the goat took to the boy.

The father shook his head and said, "I'm going to have to get that boy a goat. I don't know what it is, but he's just crazy about goats."

When I heard that, I lit up. "How do you think he'd like to own that goat?" I offered.

"You'd give him the goat?"

"Not only give him the goat, I'd give him a bag of feed to go along."

You never saw such a happy boy. From time to time, I would meet somebody who knew the man, and I would ask about the goat. Everyone reported that the boy and the goat were inseparable. That was one of those cases where everybody won.

Equipping the Home Office

When we were first building our house and hospital. I didn't have any equipment. The war in the Pacific was over, and there were huge quantities of used medical equipment being sold at auction. We were located about ten miles from the Quonset Naval Air Station, one of the biggest bases on the Atlantic coast, and home to the famous Construction Battalions of the Seabees who originated there (where the term "Quonset Hut" originated).

A huge sale of used military equipment, including medical supplies, was advertised, with qualified veterans to receive preference in the bidding. I registered for the sale, presented my discharge papers, and received a number. But it soon became obvious that young veterans with legitimate discharge papers were there to provide cover for some civilian dealers, and, when the bidding started, these people proceeded to gobble up all the equipment.

The equipment was arranged in large numbered lots, so it wasn't a question of picking out individual pieces that a small timer like me would be able to bid on. After I'd observed a few hours of this bidding from which I had been excluded, I approached the auctioneer. I explained to him that I felt that this whole process was rigged and that the individual veteran didn't have a chance of getting any of this equipment. I told him I was going to get in touch with the adjutant general, and I dropped a few other names of people I knew in the administration at Quonset.

That was enough for him to say, "Is there any particular equipment that you are interested in?"

"Yes, there is, but it's not in individual lots, so I had no chance."

"Go around and pick out all the equipment that you are interested in and put it in a pile. We'll number that pile, and we'll see that you are able to get what you want."

I had a young man with me who had a truck. He and I proceeded to pick out all kinds of medical, veterinary, and dental surplus, and instruments, sterilizers, hoof knives, overhead lights, and six castle lights still packed in their boxes. I picked stainless steel tables and cabinets, and we were busy pushing it all around until we had a very large pile. During a lull, I told the auctioneer that I had gathered the things that I was interested in. He came over to the pile, put a number on it, and asked, "Now, you've got everything in there that you are interested in?"

"Yes, sir. I've got everything I want." There were enough things in there to equip several veterinary hospitals.

The bidding started again and he called out my lot number. He announced it as a mixed assortment and proceeded to open the bid even though no one had had a chance to preview the pile. Somebody opened with $50 and another person said $75; quickly it went up to $200, and then I bid $210. "Sold," said the auctioneer. He pointed at me, and I had all this beautiful equipment.

It took a full pickup load to get it all, which constituted most of the equipment in my office; a lot of it went to four other veterinary practices in Rhode Island. Years later, I gave away an overhead castle light still in its original wooden box, packed and wrapped, glittering as if it had just come from the factory. That would have cost a couple thousand dollars. Dr. Bruzzi has it in his surgery room.

In addition to the equipment, they were selling used Jeeps. I bought one in beautiful condition for a little over $100. At the farm, I attached a huge rake arrangement to it, and my wife rode in back and raised and lowered this contraption so that we could clear our land. We used that rig to do all the rough work and we saved some money.

My First Big Venture

Once I was in practice for myself, I had a chance to make what was then a princely sum in my first business deal. A dairy farmer named Harold "Skee" Covell had a beautiful, high-producing herd of Holstein cows at his farm, Jingle Valley, in West Kingston. He wanted to acquire half a dozen Jersey cows, which were not very heavy milk producers as far as quantity, but they would raise the butterfat level to meet the minimum requirements at the time. He knew I was acquainted with dairy farmers around the state and asked me if I knew where he could get some Jerseys.

"Well, Harold, I take care of one of the premier Jersey farms in the country, owned by a very wealthy man by the name of Fortune Ryan." Ryan owned what was called a Vaucluse Jersey farm in Newport, across Narragansett Bay. To get there back then, you had to go over a bridge to Jamestown Island, and then take a ferry to Newport.

I was well acquainted with the herd. The stock was continually being upgraded, and any animals that didn't conform to standard would be sold at auction. I called the herdsman and asked him if they had any Jersey cows that could be purchased. He told me that they were culling a number of their less valuable cows, which would be available for sale. I selected six young Jerseys, examined them to make sure they were pregnant, and thought these cows would be exactly what my client would want. The herdsman told me that they would cost $500 each. (I intended to charge Harold $600.)

The problem was that I had to arrange for the cows to be transported from Newport to Jingle Valley Farm. I called a friend who had a cattle truck, and he said he'd be glad to help. When

I asked him how much he would charge me, he told me that I didn't have to pay, that I'd been good to him.

I asked my wife to make out a check to the farm for $3,000. "As soon as I get the cows over to Harold, he'll give me $3,600 and we'll have a nice $600 profit." She thought that I should take the cows over to Mr. Covell, and then, after he'd paid me, go back to Ryan's farm and give them their money.

I disagreed, "That's just not the way it's done."

"Well, suppose Harold Covell refuses to accept the cows when you deliver them? Then what are you going to do?" After a rather heated argument, she finally said, "Well, I hope you know what you're doing, because if you lose all this money that we've worked so hard to save, we're going to be in bad shape."

I finally had my way, had the check to pay for the cows, and delivered them to Harold Covell. When those cows were unloaded from the van and paraded into his barn with his whole family there, he just kept shaking his head, saying, "These are the most beautiful cows. I really thank you for getting them for me." He asked me to come into his milk room, where he cooled and kept his milk, and paid me the $3,600. Then he counted out $500 extra for my trouble. That was my first big score, my first big venture, and, needless to say, my wife and I celebrated that night. We often talked about our reluctance to part with that money that we had saved so carefully.

Johnny and the Animals

Johnny Corrects the Teacher

I was still working for the federal government when my first child, John, was born. By the time he was old enough to go to preschool, I was in private practice and would take him on calls with me as often as I could. My wife and I used to take turns picking him up.

One day, the teacher met me at the door and told me she had a funny story for me. It was getting close to Christmas time and they were having a class discussion about Santa's reindeer. One of the children wanted to know where reindeer came from and the teacher tried to explain how animals are born, with a birds-and-bees kind of thing. At that point Johnny started laughing, so the teacher said to him, "Johnny, stand up and tell the class what you find so funny about this." He was reluctant, but she urged him on.

Johnny told the class that I had taken him with me on a call to help with a cow that was having trouble calving. "My father put me in the car and took me over there. And while I was there watching, my father reached inside the cow and in a little while he pulled the little calf out."

I remember the incident. Johnny was just standing there, wide-eyed with amazement. After we cleaned up and were on the way home, he asked me how that calf got in there. He wasn't old enough for me to explain, but he was curious and persistent. I had to tell him something, so I said, "Well, the mother and the father have to get together." That was part of my son's experience. Later, he assisted me in the office and witnessed so many things.

Johnny Gets a Raise in Pay

In the beginning, I never had any help in the office, except for my wife and my boys as they got older. I had my older boy, John, help me do surgery in the evenings. As part of his allowance, I agreed to give him a dollar for every surgery that he helped me with, and he helped me for quite a while. One night, my wife said that she wanted to talk to me, that Johnny was very upset.

"He asked you for a raise in pay. He said that you had raised your prices and he felt that he should be getting two dollars."

I said I thought that one dollar was enough, and she disagreed. Needless to say, I not only paid him two dollars, but I ended up paying him five before he went off to school. Later, I hired a high school teacher who was interested in animal surgery; he would call every day to see if I had scheduled any surgery, because it gave him a chance to observe and make some extra money. That went on for quite a while.

Chris, the Wonder Dog

My son John reminded me to tell the story about Chris, the Wonder Dog. I had read about this dog; that he had appeared on television; he was a mixed mongrel dog that could communicate with his owner. Right after the TV show, the owner called to say that, all of a sudden, the dog had stopped communicating and he just wouldn't answer his owner's questions, so could I take a look at him? When he came in for the appointment, my son happened to be there. He was only about twelve years old, and he had some treats in his pocket. He gave one to Chris and patted him. Chris wagged his tail and Johnny gave him another one.

The owner exclaimed, "Boy, he's really taking to your son. Ask him some questions, Johnny. See if you can communicate with him." The dog would communicate by tapping your arm with his paw; one tap meant yes and two meant no.

"Is your name King?" Johnny asked. Two taps.

Then, "Is your name Jim?" Two taps.

Johnny tried three or four more names. Finally, he asked, "Is your name Chris?" The dog was all excited. He tapped once.

Then they started actually communicating, and Johnny said things to him like, "Chris, how much is two plus two?" And Chris would tap four times. It looked to me that the owner might be sending signals. So I asked him to go to another part of the house where Chris wouldn't be able to see him. Chris and Johnny had a great time talking. Johnny asked, "Chris, we have a horse running this Saturday and he's named after me, Go John Go. Is he going to win?" And Chris tapped twice, no. Then, he asked, "Is he going to finish second?" Chris tapped once, yes. And that's where he finished, second.

In the meantime, I solved Chris's problem. After that, Chris started communicating again for his owner.

Johnny's Horse

When my son Johnny was about ten years old, he realized that young people around here had their own horses and competed in the different shows. He decided that he wanted to have a horse of his own too, and asked if I would get him one. I told him I would but I had to be convinced that he would take care of him, ride him, groom him, feed him, and clean up the tack, and really spend some time with him.

I ran into a beautiful, young gray horse that had been tried on the racetrack and was found to be too slow for racing. This was a big, impressive, well-muscled, gentle horse, a Thorough-bred. I decided that this would be a good horse for Johnny, and I bought him. For the first six months, Johnny was beside himself with joy, and he took care of the horse and went down to the stable every day.

At the time, Martha Watson was working for me. Martha was particularly bright, and an exceptionally good rider from the time she arrived, at about the age of sixteen. One day, she was preparing to give Johnny a lesson, but as she was putting the horse through his paces the horse stopped suddenly and refused to go forward. Martha tried everything. The horse absolutely refused to move; Martha just couldn't get him to do anything.

After about five minutes, Johnny hollered at her, "Give him his head and push forward on him."

I said, "Look, don't be giving Martha any advice. You are just learning and you can wait until it's your turn." Johnny waited a minute or more and the horse still wouldn't move and he started at Martha again. I said to John, "You're such a wise guy and you know all about riding, I'll bet you my ten dollars against your nickel that you can't make this horse move. Get up on the horse and let's see how smart you are."

We put him on the horse. He adjusted the stirrups, picked up the reins, clucked to the horse, touched his side, and off the horse went. He galloped around one way, and then the other way. When he got off the horse, he put out his hand and said, "Pay me."

"Pay you? I'll tell you what you can do. You can take it out of what you owe me."

With that, Johnny started up to the house crying, to his mother. When I got home, my wife said to me, "Is it true what Johnny said?"

"Yes. It's true, he's getting to be a real wise guy and talking out of turn."

"But you told him you'd give him ten dollars if he could make the horse move."

"Well, it was just a figure of speech. I'm not paying him." Well, for the next three or four days that's all I heard about: I hadn't kept my word and that's not right. Finally, I said, "It's easier to give him the ten dollars than to have to listen to this for the rest of my life. Whatever he did and whatever he and that horse communicated sure made a fool out of me."

After several months, Johnny developed other interests. He wasn't taking care of his horse or riding him. I got after him. I told him he could be a champion with this horse and win a lot of the Class A shows around here, and if he didn't take care of this horse and ride him, I would have to sell him. So he said he would, but he lost interest again.

I put an ad in the *Virginia Chronicle*, a big horse newspaper where people advertised horses for sale. The phone started ringing. I said he was a green horse, but he was almost seventeen hands tall, had excellent conformation, could jump like a deer, wasn't afraid of any big jumps, and was easy to handle. One of the first calls I got was from a woman in Far Hills, New Jersey. She said that she was very interested in the horse and asked how much I wanted for him I said I wanted $5,000, a lot of money at that time. She asked where we were located and we agreed to meet at the Westerly airport.

In flew a beautiful twin-engine plane, which turned out to be her own plane. I drove her to the farm and took the horse out. She was very impressed with him. She said she'd like to see him jump. Martha Watson was there that day, so I said, "Okay, Martha, tack him up, and we'll take him out where the jumps are set up." The jumps were set at about five feet high at the top of the stanchions. Martha took the horse around the field and he cleared those jumps like they were nothing.

"I've seen enough, and now I'd like to get on him, if you don't mind. And I would like you to lower those fences; they're too high." She got up on the horse and made a couple of turns around the field. She dismounted and got out her checkbook and said, "He's a nice horse. I'll take him." The horse went down to her farm in New Jersey, and within a year, he was on the United States Olympic Jumping Team. He went on to have a very successful career as an open jumper. I kept my word. I had gotten Johnny a good horse, and it worked out very well.

The Ladd School

The Ladd School was a huge compound in Exeter, Rhode Island, not far from where I live. It was for mentally handicapped people and was run by a Dr. Ladd, who was really progressive, recognizing that the residents should not be locked up or treated inhumanely. He instituted athletic programs, activities, and entertainment. There was vaudeville every weekend, when various entertainers and comedians would go there and perform. One of the entertainers told me that the reason he went there was that, no matter what he did, he got a standing, screaming ovation. As a performer, that was the best pay he could get, from people who appreciated his tricks, like pulling pigeons out of a hat.

My contact with the residents was through the dairy barn, which contained over a hundred prize Holstein cattle. It was run entirely by a dairyman/herdsman with the help of the residents at the school. During that time, I met quite a few of the boys, and somehow, when word got around that I was coming, they would all gather at the dairy barn to meet me. They knew that I would stop on the way and buy cigarettes for them (this was before 1964, when the Surgeon General's *Report on Smoking and Health* came out).

First thing, I would walk over to the group waiting for the cigarettes. In charge of the entire group was a tall boy they called Brownie because of the color of his skin. I would always give the cigarettes to Brownie to distribute; Brownie was very reliable and fair. One day, Brownie took me aside and told me, very seriously, "Doctor, I appreciate your bringing the cigarettes, but next time, would you buy the king size? They don't cost any more and there are twenty-two more puffs in the king size than in a regular cigarette."

That floored me. "Brownie, I never knew that." Needless to say, from that point on, I bought the king-size cigarettes.

At the barn there was a young man in charge of the milking machines and changing the machines on every cow. I would watch him work, and he was quite good. I never really knew what was wrong with him, so I asked the herdsman, a fellow named Abbott, "Why is Mason here?"

"Well, Mason has these spells; he goes berserk when we send him out to work on the farm. He's a good worker, but when the full moon comes, he goes completely out of his head and can't be controlled. He acts like a wild man, and that's why he won't be let out."

I was there to test the cows for mastitis, an infection of the udder. The way that you test for it is to bottle and label a sample of milk from each teat. The samples were then taken to the state laboratories and tested to make sure that there were no bacteria. While Mason was helping me with the bottles, he asked, "Doctor, what are you doing?"

"I'm testing the cows for mastitis, Mason."

"Mastitis. What's that?"

"Well, it's something that is caused by a bug. This particular bug is very hard to catch, and if I could ever capture it, it would be worth a lot of money." He wanted to know what the bug looked like, so I said, "Have you seen a tomato worm? Well, it looks like one of those tomato worms, but the difference is that tomato worms have green eyes and this bug that I'm looking for has pink eyes. So, if you ever see one come out of the udder and then duck right back in again, you try to catch it. I'll leave a jar up on the shelf for you, and if you find any, call me right away."

He said he would. The next time I came back, the herdsman wanted to know, "What's this about a bug you have Mason looking for?" So I told him, and he said, "Well, it keeps him occupied and that's okay."

One Sunday, I got a call from the school that there was a cow down with milk fever. My father was visiting from Pennsylvania and we went over in his car. I told him, "Willie is always over there when it's cigarette time. The boy is an expert on license plates. He can't read, but they say he can identify every license plate in the country. So we'll be there with your Pennsylvania license plate, and we'll see how good this boy is." We stopped, bought the cigarettes, and went through the usual distribution routine.

Meantime, Willie had been walking around my father's car looking at the license plate. I said, "Willie, you're pretty good on license plates. Suppose you tell me what state this license plate comes from." I started in with my father's car, "This license plate comes from New York."

"No, New York is yellow and black."

Then I named New Jersey, then Delaware, and half a dozen more. He gave the colors and the backgrounds for every one, and my father was impressed. Finally, I called out Pennsylvania, and Willie grinned. "Yes, Pennsylvania." He gave me the colors, and then he came over, got real close to me, and said, "Doctor. I'm supposed to be a fool. That's why I'm in here, but I'm not stupid."

Well, my father couldn't get over half the boys there. He couldn't understand, after seeing them work and talk, why they were there, but, of course, they all had their problems.

The Flood

Another day, during a dry spell, I went to the Ladd School to check on the cows as usual. But as I drove in, I saw that the street was full of water. As I entered the dairy barn, I asked, "Did you have a flood, Adam?"

"We had a flood from the water tank. We were cleaning out the hen houses, starting on the top floor, and I had a crew of boys with me. Up there we have a big steel drum that we were filling with water, so we could add disinfectant and scrub everything. We started filling the tub when I got a telephone call to go to the office, and I told the boys to keep an eye on the drum until I got back."

Adam was held up for about two hours, and on his way back to the hen house, he noticed the water running down the street. He ran up to the third floor, and there were four of five boys, all standing around the steel drum, feet soaking wet, pants soaking wet, some with pants rolled up, and all of them keeping their eye on the tub. Nobody had moved. Those were the orders. "It was my fault," said Adam.

Deputizing the Boys

The Ladd School stories remind me of some fun I had with two neighborhood boys when I first lived in Kingston. Across the street from me was a family named LaFrance. The father was in the agronomy department at the college, and he had a son named Rudy, who was about ten years old. He later went to West Point and, for all I know, may be a general by now. Next door was a boy named Herbie Brooks, whose father was in the English department. When these boys saw my government car, they came over to the house and introduced themselves. They were curious about what kind of work I was doing.

"If I tell you, you must be sworn to secrecy. My cover here is to be at the agricultural school, but I'm really a secret FBI agent and I need help. We have received a report of a German spy residing in Kingston." I deputized both boys; I told them that this was top-secret stuff and that if I found out that they were divulging any of my secrets, I would have to un-deputize them. Using a picture from a magazine, I identified the man, who might be wearing a disguise. I would expect them to keep their eyes and ears open and report to me every night. As soon as the boys spotted my car pulling into the driveway, they would come over to give their daily report, that they were still actively looking out for the spy and they hadn't told their parents about their assignment.

Jack Morgan

Jack Morgan, a former prize fighter, ran the Top of the Hill restaurant, a small truck stop and bar in Hope Valley on a two-lane road, then the main route to New York. Once the trucks got to the top of the hill, they would park at the side of the road and rest or spend some time in the restaurant. The food was excellent home cooking prepared by Jack's wife, Rosa.

Jack was a sportsman, in particular, a fighter. He had also wrestled professionally, but boxing was his sport. I was interested in boxing, having boxed on the Penn State team; I maintained a life-long interest in boxing. Jack and I had many discussions about boxing, and there was a large, enthusiastic crowd of fight followers in the area. There were some small fight clubs in Providence, but if you made it to the Rhode Island Auditorium, well, that was the big time. Some world-class fighters were there during that time, and Jack and I went to the fights on a regular basis.

One fighter I saw, the one that most people will remember, was Rocky Marciano, who would become the undefeated world heavyweight champion. He started his career in Providence, and Jack and I attended every one of his fights. He was a devastating fighter. He was built like a brick wall. He could take the hardest punch from any heavyweight and not blink. He refused to back up for anybody. He would get his opponent in a corner and demolish him. He was crude when he started, but people went absolutely crazy for Rocky.

After Rocky had won about fifteen rights in a row, he was talked about as the Great White Hope. He was not only white, he was Italian. Rocky was building his record on a bunch of heavyweights who had no chance against him, so we had a lot of opportunities around New England to watch a future world champion. About this time, he arranged a fight with a journeyman, an old pro who knew all the tricks, named Ted "Tiger" Lowry, from Connecticut. Tiger was put in there as just one more person to fatten Rocky's record.

Tiger was a regular visitor at the Top of the Hill restaurant. When Jack found out that Tiger had been matched with Rocky to fight at the Rhode Island Auditorium, he couldn't wait to introduce me. He got us ringside seats. Tiger was a veteran of hundreds of fights. He'd been in with the best. He was a clever boxer, knew how to absorb punches, and knew how to take them on his elbows. He was a very shifty mover, so that to catch him flatfooted or in a position where you could inflict some damage was nearly impossible.

I had never seen Tiger fight, but Jack assured me that Rocky was going to have his hands full. The fight began, and through the first five rounds, Rocky never laid a glove on Tiger. Tiger danced, he shuffled, he moved, he bobbed, he weaved, he tied Rocky up. He did the thing that Muhammad Ali (Cassius Clay, as we knew him) would later call rope-a-dope. Through five rounds, Marciano had not landed a solid punch, and Tiger was way ahead on points.

This was a ten-round fight, and Rocky's handlers started to panic. This would not do. Besides, Rocky had not sat on his stool during the entire fight, but was kicking the ropes, punching the posts, and hollering at his handlers, his people. Who had gotten this person in there with him, someone he couldn't touch? At the end of the sixth round with Tiger way ahead, no matter how prejudiced the judges were, there was absolutely no way that Rocky had won a round. At ringside, we noticed two or three strangers come over and talk to Tiger's handlers; there was quite a discussion and when the bell rang, Tiger proceeded to dance for the remaining rounds, never even jabbing Marciano. Marciano was earning points, even though he was only hitting Tiger's forearms or side and was landing only glancing headshots. That was the first time anyone had gone the distance with Rocky. Rocky went on to become world champion and and much more polished compared to the way he behaved that day.

On the way home, Jack said to me, "Boy, old Tiger could've won all ten rounds if he wanted to. You better believe that they were making some kind of deal with him. I'm going to call him." Tiger wasn't about to tell Jack about it on the telephone, so Jack insisted that Tiger come to the restaurant for dinner because we wanted the real scoop. We met in the back room. Jack leaned over and to Tiger and said, "Just between us guys, now, what happened?"

"Jack, within a few weeks, they are going to announce a big fight. I am going to get with another up-and-coming young white fighter, and it's gonna be the biggest pay night of my life. I never made over $1,000. I'm going out there and that is my reward."

Sure enough, the fight was announced. Tiger fought this other white boy, as he called him. It was a shame because Tiger, as Brando said in the movie *On the Waterfront*, "coudda been a contender." In fact, Tiger was the only one to go up against Rocky Marciano and last ten rounds against him not once but twice.

Jack was a drinker all his life, but I never saw him when he wasn't in control of himself until late one evening, on my way home from a call. I decided I needed a cup of coffee, and Jack's restaurant sometimes stayed open past midnight.

I found Jack behind the bar with some people. He came out to greet me. He wrapped his arms around my body, lifted me up, and proceeded to squeeze me with a wrestling hold; he was like a piece of iron, a little Rocky Marciano. He was very muscular, short, and tough. I used to tell him that he looked like the little Manassas Mauler, old Jack Dempsey. All of a sudden, I couldn't catch my breath. I tried to kick at him to let me go, but because he was on the sauce, he didn't realize right away that I was gasping. Finally he let me down. I sat on a stool for a while, having difficulty catching my breath, and I knew that he had cracked some of my ribs.

I called him every name I could think of. "You rotten so and so. You'll never see me again." I walked out of there, got in my car, and went home. I had my ribs taped and was in a great deal of pain for quite a while.

When Jack realized what he had done, he called, and my wife said I didn't want to talk to him. He kept calling. Then he came over and he started talking to me. "Look," I said, "I don't want anything to do with you anymore. When you're drinking, you're out of control, and one of these days, you are going to kill yourself or somebody else." That broke his heart, but I told him, "That's it. I'm done with you." He went away crestfallen. This went on for about a month.

Then he showed up one day. "Doc," he said, " I know what I did and you were right about my drinking—I could have killed you, I guess. It's been a bad month for me, you know, the way you feel, and I realize how wrong I was." He said that he had been to see an old priest at his church in Hope Valley, and that the priest had advised him to take the Pledge, which is intended to help people abstain from alcohol. According to Jack, he was supposed to give up something that he particularly loved. Jack's favorite thing in all the world was ice cream. He could eat it by the gallon. So he told the priest he would give up ice cream. It sounds funny now, but that's just the way it happened. He died at age eighty-two or eighty-three, and he never had another spoonful of ice cream. Jack was a man of his word.

Jack would do anything for me, and on several occasions, he asked me if I could do something for him, which I always did. The horse I named after Jack finished third in the New England Futurity—a great source of pride for Jack, who was also an avid horseplayer.

Orville Watts

When I came to Wakefield, I heard about James O. Watts from many sources. Everybody called him by his middle name, Orville. He was the principal judge in our county courthouse in West Kingston. He also had a law practice in Wakefield (there were one or two other lawyers in town but he got most of the business). His law office was on Main Street. Right next to him was Phil, the barber. Judge Watts was an unforgettable character. He was very tall, had a prominent Adam's apple, and he wore a string necktie.

Most of the professional people in Wakefield, whether they were lawyers, doctors, or dentists, were engaged in some form of farming. Judge Watts raised prize sheep and prize chickens and drove Standardbred horses around town, and on the beach—horse and wagon; he loved to race. This area was once known for a strain of Standardbred horses, the Narragansett Pacers, and Judge Watts was well known in the Standardbred organization. Trotting and pacing races developed here and money changed hands on the outcome. Other people around here were knowledgeable about Standardbreds, one of them being Jim Caffrey, who married into the Kenyon family, owners of the only department store in town.

Every year the Judge went to Harrisburg, Pennsylvania, to the Standardbred auction. That was his vacation. It was the biggest sale in the country for Standardbred horses at that time. The Judge would sit in the front row and read the auction catalogs, never looking up, and bid on every horse that came into the auction ring.

The rules of the auction were that the opening bid would be accepted, and the auction would go on from there. It was generally assumed that if a horse came into the ring, the nature of its conformation and pedigree would likely bring a sum in the neighborhood of $10,000. As soon as the auctioneer read the pedigree and went through the whole genealogy of the horse, he would ask for the opening bid. The Judge would raise his hand and bid $100. Some other comedian would say $200, somebody else would say $250, and the horse would end up selling for $10,000 or more.

Needless to say, the Judge became a pain in the neck to these people. But one time the Judge was successful in one of his bids. He called me to come to his farm to see the Standardbred that he had just bought at the sale, a caricature of a horse. He was a bag of bones, with a sway back, long ears, and great big knees. He reminded me of James Earle Fraser's sculpture *The End of the Trail.* I was amazed that the Judge would buy a horse of obviously faulty conformation, which didn't look like much of any kind of horse that anybody, particularly a supposed connoisseur of horseflesh, would buy.

"What do you think of him, Doctor?" the Judge inquired.

"Well, Judge, it's hard to tell."

Later on, I went downtown to Jim Caffrey's store and told him about my visit with Judge Watts. Jim convulsed with laughter and when he asked what I thought of the horse, I said, "That's a pretty poor looking horse."

Jim told me that the auction company had conspired to find this horse and include him in the catalog and the sale. They knew that the Judge would listen to the spiel—the longer the spiel, the better the pedigree. It went on for nearly five minutes, and the Judge didn't even look at the horse in the ring. He raised his hand and said, "$100." And the auctioneer said, "Sold." That's how the Judge got that horse. He never admitted to what really happened and finally managed to get the horse to pull a cart, but he always referred to him as the champion that he bought at the Standardbred sale in Harrisburg.

The Judge had quite a collection of farm animals, and although his legal fees were reasonable, he was known for his parsimony. His law clients thought he was "pretty expensive, but he's good." The Judge didn't call me unless it was really necessary.

One day, I was at the barbershop for a haircut (which, as I recall, was fifty cents). Afterwards, I walked down the hall past the Judge's office. The door happened to be open, so I poked my head in and waved and said hello.

"I just got a haircut, Judge, and I was walking along down the hall when I reminded myself that I had a question for you. I have some horses up at my barn, and young Martha Watson gallops and trains one for me. A couple of weeks ago, she had her girlfriend over when I wasn't there; she put her friend on this horse and the girl fell off and broke her ankle. It occurred to me that I might get sued."

"Oh, what kind of horse was it?"

"A jumping horse, a Thoroughbred,"

"Has the horse ever hurt or dumped anybody before?"

"No."

"Well, you know every dog is entitled to one bite, and I don't see how you could be liable."

"That's good. I didn't think so, but I'm relieved." Then, as an afterthought, I asked, "Do I owe you anything, Judge?"

He leaned back in his chair with a kind of expansive look and said, "Oh, I guess ten dollars will take care of it." Well, that staggered me. I had just gotten a haircut for fifty cents and here's the Judge asking me for ten dollars for this five-minute conversation. I paid, but I thought to myself, "I'll get even, Judge."

The opportunity arose about a month later when I came home from making calls and my wife said, "I just got a call from Judge Watts's wife and she's all in a panic. Her husband purchased a champion ram lamb at the Eastern States Exhibition, and when she went out to check on the lamb she found him on the floor, breathing hard, and unable to get up. He asked her to find out if you could get over there." I told my wife, "This is my chance," and I shot over there.

The ram lamb was obviously in a great deal of distress. He had put his head through the feeding creep and in trying to pull his head out had gotten caught. In his struggle, he had thrown himself on his side and had become bloated. Simply relieving the gas would take care of him, but I told Mrs. Watts it was serious. I advised her to go to the house and call the Judge while I got to work in the barn. While she was gone, I picked up the ram, put his head between my legs, and kept hitting his side until he burped and the gas came up. As soon as I relieved the bloat, he was fine.

Then I proceeded to take out all the drugs I had in my medical bag and line them up. Mrs. Watts came back into the barn to say that the Judge was on his way. When she saw the ram was standing up, she asked what had happened. I said, "Well, Mrs. Watts, I gave him everything I had.

"It's a miracle, Dr. Kaplan."

"It's a good thing I got here when I did."

About five minutes later, the Judge arrived. I said, "Judge, we had some real trouble here, but luckily I was able to get here in time and save him."

"What in the world do you think happened?"

I told him that I thought it might have been from the hay the Judge had picked up along the road and fed to the ram—some kind of poison was probably used to kill the weeds. "I had to give him all kinds of antidotes."

He saw all the bottles lined up and said, "Oh, thank God. I wouldn't have wanted to lose that lamb." We stood there and talking for a while, and then he said, "Come on into the house and I'll pay you."

He opened his big roll-top desk and took out his checkbook. In his flourishing, beautiful hand he wrote my name and then looked up at me through his pince-nez glasses, the kind of half-glasses that sit at the end of your nose, and said, "How much will that be, Doctor?"

I looked at him, explaining that I'd used a lot of drugs, and that twenty-five dollars would take care of it—just the way he had said "Oh, that'll be ten dollars" to me. The Judge got my message. He gave me the twenty-five dollars, and by the look he gave me, I knew he would never call me again. Sure enough, he never did.

The Landed Gentry

Even though the dairy farmers were the backbone of my practice early on, there were also some wealthy landowners who had animals on their estates in the area. One was a young woman named Ann Kenyon (her mother was a member of the Knight family that goes back to the old textile mills). Ann was an avid outdoorswoman, did swordfishing, and had flown airplanes during World War II, ferrying them across to Europe. People said that she could hold her own wrestling a man. She had a beautiful farm and among her prize possessions was a flock of Southdown sheep. She was a world-class equestrian, having been instructed from the time she was a little girl by Dick Grant, who came from England. Dick was my friend and always kept me up to date about what was happening at the Kenyon farms.

Ann was hard to get along with. She knew what she wanted and was opinionated and arrogant in many ways. She was a member of the so-called aristocracy down here at that time—people from New York and other places sailed in on their yachts and had their polo ponies. As I was the only veterinarian in the area, these people became my clients. During all the years that I practiced, I put up with a lot of things. One hot summer day, we were worming and inoculating a flock of sheep at the Kenyon place. We were having problems catching and holding the sheep, and Ann and I exchanged some words. At that point, I had had just about enough of her arrogance and I told her to get herself another veterinarian. With that, I got in the car and went home.

Shortly after that, I was over at Bayfield Farm, a very fine Holstein farm run by George and Helen Causey, and Helen said,

"I heard that you and Ann had a run-in. Now she's talking to all of her friends, and she's proposing to get another veterinarian to come in here. She wants everybody to get together and form an organization to set someone up."

I didn't hear any more of it until one day when I was down at my stable with a mare and her new foal and someone came up to the door. It was Ann Kenyon.

"Hello, Martin, I heard you had a new foal, and I was just going by and I thought I'd stop in to see it," as if absolutely nothing had happened, and I became her veterinarian again.

A year or so later, Ann told me about a friend of hers named Marjorie McLean, who had a big farm in Connecticut with beautiful stables. Mrs. McLean was known in the United States for having the finest Hackney ponies in the world, and the people who lived on her property showed these ponies all over the country.

Ann told me that Mrs. McLean had bought a big estate in Wakefield. She would be building barns for her Hackneys and was concerned that her veterinarian in Connecticut would not be able to take care of them here because it was too far. So Ann had told Mrs. McLean about me, and I told Ann, "Sure, if she builds her stable and wants me to take care of her ponies, I'd be glad to." I knew the veterinarian who had been taking care of her stable in Connecticut, and I called him. "She's hard to get along with," he warned me.

The McLean barns were being constructed, and I heard that the horses were going to be moving in soon. I was up in West Greenwich taking care of some wild cattle when my wife took a call. When I got home, my wife said to me, "Who is Mrs. McLean? She called this afternoon and wanted you to come right away to see an old stallion having trouble with a bad tooth. I told her that you would not be coming home till about five o'clock. She wanted to know the name and the telephone number of the farm in West Greenwich where you were working. And when I told her that I couldn't give out the number, she was really rude and slammed down the phone."

I'd been home a little while and the phone rang. It was Mrs. McLean again. I interrupted her. "Mrs. McLean, before you go any further, I want to tell you something. I don't know you and you don't know me. I'm not hard to get along with, but you demanded to know where I was, and you slammed down the phone on my wife after telling her that when you call somebody you expect them to be there. So I need to get something straight with you. If you are going to be that way with me, you can get another vet." I hung up on her.

Fifteen minutes later the phone rang again, "Dr. Kaplan, this is Mrs. McLean, would you please come down and see me?"

"Mrs. McLean, you just said the magic word."

"I what?"

"You said 'please.' I'll just have a bite to eat and I'll be right down." So I went down and took care of her stallion, and I didn't have any more trouble from Mrs. McLean. She knew where I was coming from and vice versa. We got along just fine for a number of years until she passed away and the estate was dispersed.

Jack Turco, M.D.

When the young surgeon Jack Turco came here to practice, this community was a playground for the wealthy. Like Newport, this side of Narragansett Bay had a large summer population with their mansions and their private club open only to White Anglo-Saxon Protestants, and no bones about it. In order to become a member, you had to be approved by a committee.

Dr. Turco made house calls to these people during the summer. He was an excellent golfer (he was also an excellent athlete, All-American at Georgetown), and he decided at some point that he wanted to join the club. One of his patients sponsored him, but he was turned down because he was Italian. So he told them, "Well, if I'm not good enough to be in your club, then I'm not good enough to be your doctor." That created an uproar because they really depended on him. Eventually, he was accepted.

Groucho Marx had a great line about not being accepted: "I don't care to belong to a club that accepts people like me as members." Things have certainly improved. I've now lived long enough to see both a woman and an African-American running in the Democratic Party's primaries as presidential candidates and another woman the Republican Party's nominee for vice president of the United States.

As I said, Dr. Turco was a great athlete and sports enthusiast, and he loved horses. I admired the work of "Virginia" Robinson, a good, old-time trainer from Virginia, an excellent horseman. There was an occasion when a horse trained by Virginia Robinson was running in Maryland at the Laurel Park Race Track.

The horse had a good chance to win, so I called Dr. Turco and we went down to Maryland.

With the first race, Dr. Turco and Robinson started what is called a "show parlay." You bet on a horse: it could be the favorite but must come in at least third. If you did well enough on several races in a row, the winnings would accumulate. The horse we were interested in was entered in the seventh race, and by that time Jack Turco and Virginia Robinson had had quite a bit of success. They bet the entire amount on the horse and the horse won.

It had started to snow. By evening it was coming down pretty hard, and there was no way that we could drive home. The highways were all blocked, so we decided to stay at a hotel and play cards. We all had quite a pile of money from the day's winnings. There was a party going on in the adjoining suite, and all of a sudden we heard, "Is there a doctor anywhere?"

It turned out that one of the leading jockeys in the country had cut his instep on a broken bottle, and it was bleeding profusely. Dr. Turco always carried an emergency kit that included local anesthesia and some drugs. He popped right over there, went to work, and sewed up the jockey's foot. After some months, the jockey regained his form and was riding in all the big stake races around the country. When asked about his renewed riding success, he said that he had been in a bit of a slump, so he changed his riding style by lowering one stirrup—it's called riding acey/deucey—and it had made all the difference in his balance on the horse. But we all knew the real reason.

My Friend Mike Hudson, Jr.

Not many years after I started in practice, I got a call from one of the big estate owners on Ocean Road in Narragansett asking if I would make a house call, which I normally didn't do for household pets. There was a very sick dog that could not be moved, so I put my young son Johnny in the car and we went to see if we could do anything for the little dog.

I pulled into the driveway of a huge mansion and was escorted into the house by a butler in a white coat. I had Johnny by the hand. A very gracious woman greeted us. "Hello, Doctor. My name is Sadie and this is my son, Mike, Jr., and this is our dog, Shorty Pie." I treated the dog. It wasn't anything serious, really. But they were very grateful and proceeded not only to give me more money than they owed me, but also a basket of toys and various things for my son, and some bottles of liquor (they didn't ask me whether or not I drank), and some eggs and fruit. That began a long friendship and association with Mike Hudson, Jr., who was exactly my age. Our birthdays were within a couple of weeks of each other.

Mike Hudson, Jr., was a savant. At that time, not many people knew what a savant was, including me; some people wrongly said retarded. But Mike would continually amaze me with some of the things he would do.

Mike and Sadie and Sadie's second huband, Pat Cummings, were animal lovers. (Sadie and Mike's father, Mike Hudson, Sr., had owned a chain of department stores in the South.) As I got to know them all, I could tell there was something wrong with Mike Jr., but I wasn't sure what. If I happened to be there for lunch, I would see Mike in another room doing jigsaw puzzles. The *New York Times* would be lying there all rumpled up. I said,

"Do you read the *New York Times*, Mike?" When I asked him a question about some foreign news, he quoted right out of the newspaper. I was starting to conclude that Mike had a lot of things going for him, and whatever his problem, I would probably find out.

One day, Sadie asked if I would stop by the house, pick up Mike, and take him on calls with me; she thought it would help him to develop and see different people and things. Mike didn't have to work; in theory, he was an executive in the family business. He had graduated from a military school, where his mother had met his stepfather. They were wonderful people. They never bought Mike anything that they didn't buy for me: a new jacket, new boots, new coveralls.

Mike became my constant companion. I would drive to his house and blow the horn. He'd be looking out the window and would run down the steps; we would wave to Sadie, and go off to the farm calls. During these farm calls, Mike and I would talk about different things. I would say, "Hey, Mike, how are you in math?"

"Well, pretty good."

"Do you want to play some math games?"

"Sure."

"Okay. I'll go first. How much are three and three?"

Mike would count on his fingers and he'd say, "Six."

"Right, Mike. Take away two."

He'd take away two fingers, and then he'd say, "Four."

As we rode around, we would play other games. If I asked Mike the batting average of any major league baseball player on any team, he could tell me right away. When I later looked at the paper, sure enough, he knew all the batting averages, the runs batted in, the standings of all the teams.

We even sang nursery rhymes. I would start, "Hickory Dickory Dock," and Mike would continue, "The mouse ran up the clock." It was a great way for us to have fun and he really enjoyed it. At night, I would drop him off, and he would run up the steps to where his mother would be waiting. Mike would sit down with her and recount every single call we made, everything we did, and what we ate for lunch. He didn't know the names of the medicines, but he could read the labels on the bottles and he would find the right drug. He was good company.

Lunch with Mike

We would often stop for lunch at Louis Webber's diner on Route 2 in Exeter. It was convenient to the roads I travelled, and it was the meeting place for many people like me who drove a lot. The State Police were nearby in Wickford, so we got to know a lot of the officers. Webber's specialty was a steak sandwich smothered in mushrooms that cost about two dollars. At his mother's insistence, Mike would pay for lunch every other day. She did not want me buying the lunches and would give Mike money on the day it was his turn. This arrangement was great, and it went on for at least three or four months.

One day, we weren't anywhere near Webber's, so I said to Mike, "Where do you want to eat lunch, Mike?" He said he didn't care. We were near Wakefield, where there was a little store that served hamburgers. It was my turn to pay.

The next day, I said to Mike, "We have some calls near Webber's, so let's stop there for lunch." It was his turn to pay. He started laughing.

"What's the matter, Mike?" He had a favorite expression when he did not want to tell you something; he'd say, "Nothing." I said, "Mike, you are laughing. Tell me now."

"Yesterday, I was telling Mama we were having hamburgers, and Mama said to me, 'Isn't that funny? When it's your turn to pay, you have steak sandwiches, and when it's his turn to pay, you have hamburgers.'"

Well, he was dead serious, and it occurred to me that his mother was implying that I was taking advantage of Mike. We had steak sandwiches at Webber's that day. Mike would always jump up when it was his turn. This time, I got in front of him, and said, "Mike, I'll take care of it."

"It's my turn, Doc."

"No, Mike. I'm paying today. If your mother is so worried about my cheating you, from now on I'm buying lunch." I knew that this message would get back to Sadie.

Mike went home and as usual Sadie was at the top of the stairs. We waved as usual. The next day, Mike got in the car and said, "Doc, Mama gave me orders. I have to pay for lunch today. She gave me money."

"Mike, I'm telling you and I'm telling your mother, you're not buying lunch any more."

Well, every day, Mike would get in the car and say, "Doc, please let me pay for lunch."

"No, Mike."

That entire summer, until they went back to Florida for the winter, I did not allow Mike to pay, and of course Sadie got the message and she ultimately got back at me. One day, a big truck from their department store arrived at my house. The driver had orders from Sadie to install new carpeting throughout. Out went the old; in came the new. Sadie never said a word.

Before the family left for Florida, I had a local printer make up a beautiful diploma with a big gold seal on it. The words said, "In gratitude to Mike Hudson, Jr., to recognize his valuable service as a veterinary assistant in the practice of Martin O. Kaplan," and I named all the tasks, like finding drugs, helping to restrain animals, and all the things that are necessary to be an assistant veterinarian. I signed it and my wife signed it, and we had it framed and awarded it to Mike. That became one of Mike's most treasured possessions. He carried it everywhere, and when people asked him what he did, he would take out his diploma and show them. We had a long friendship. The family dog Shorty Pie is buried in my little animal cemetery and their family minister did the honors.

Later, I named my stake horse that won the New England Futurity after Mike Hudson. And I had a really nice filly, which

I named Sadie Cummings. I also named a very good, big black horse I had after Sadie's husband, Pat Cummings.

Pat Cummings – Racer, then Jumper

I had to retire Pat Cummings after a racing injury and I brought him home. I decided that he still had a future, that I could make a jumper show horse out of him. I had quite a few horses here at my farm, which provided volunteer opportunities for several young people. It seemed that horses appealed more to girls than to boys. The girls would have their mothers ask me if they could work with the horses, groom or brush them, or take care of the saddles and tack after school. The mothers thought it was a good idea.

I had very strict rules at the stable, which I posted: no entertaining of friends, no smoking, no profane language. This was

Martha Watson on Pat Cummings at the Rocky Hill Fairgrounds about 1968 (notice that there are no "wings" on these jumps, a challenge to horse and rider who needed to keep to the center of a 41/2-ft. span while jumping over a hurdle 5' high. (Pat Cummings won the Saturday Night Fault and Out Class seven years in a row at the Rocky Hill State Fair, even when there were elephants parked next to the ring!) (Photo courtesy of Martha Watson Pena)

not a playpen, this was a place of business, and anybody who disobeyed the rules would be asked to leave. Many of those girls who started here ended up in various aspects of the horse business. Some have come back to tell me that the happiest days of their lives were here. I even heard from one way up in the wilds of Alaska, who is now a fish and wild game biologist.

When Pat Cummings was ready, I advertised him for sale. The ad described the horse as a big horse, sixteen/three hands (a hand being four inches, with the measurement taken at the shoulder, or the withers)—a big horse and a big jumper, and very desirable. I was asking $3,500, which was what I thought the horse should bring.

Sure enough, the phone started ringing shortly after I put the ad in. The first caller was a man from Cape Cod. He drove up in a beautiful Jaguar, dressed like a horseman in fancy clothes. He introduced himself and said he was here to see the horse. He was impressed with the horse and asked if he could ride him. He got his tack out of the car and put it on the horse, rode him, and asked, "What do you want for him?"

"$3,500."

"Well, that is a little too much money, but I'll give you $2,500."

"No. The price is $3,500. You are the first one who has responded to the ad and I have a bunch of other calls. That's the price. If you don't want him, probably somebody else will."

Finally, he said he would take the horse, and we shook on it.

Then he said, "Well, I'll be back tomorrow or the day after. I'll bring you a certified check for the amount, and I'd like you to prepare a written agreement that you're selling me this horse for this price."

"Well, we just shook hands on it, and I told you he's yours. We agreed."

"The way I do business, I need to have everything in writing."

"That's not the way I do business. A handshake around here is as good as a legal document."

When he said he wouldn't buy the horse without a signed agreement, I told him, "In other words, you are saying that my word is no good. Well, you have your ways of doing business," and with that I said goodbye to him and turned to Martha Watson, who was working at the barn that day.

"Martha, you've always loved this horse. Would you like to buy him?" Overwhelmed, she kind of stammered that she didn't have enough money. "Well, Martha, I'll sell him to you for a dollar, but first you need to go home and ask your father if you can have the horse and if you can keep him there where he works."

Her father was a caretaker and a chauffeur at Roland Robinson's estate in Wakefield. Rolie had a beautiful barn and horses of his own. I knew there were plenty of empty stalls, and that Rolie would give the Watsons permission to keep the horse there. When Martha's father called me, I told him, "I'd rather give the horse to Martha than sell him. He's been good to me." That was how Martha got the horse. She went on to win many championships with Pat Cummings. He became a very well-known show horse and spent a long, happy life with Martha.

Martha Watson on Pat Cummings at the Children's Services Horse Show in 1969 (photo courtesy of Martha Watson Pena)

Jim Beattie

Jim Beattie came to this country from Ireland with experience in the manufacture of lace. He shipped the machinery from England and set up his mills here in Coventry. Pretty soon he was the biggest manufacturer of lace in the United States, running his mills twenty-four hours a day. Being successful in the lace business and also a lover of Thoroughbred horses, he started a stable of very fine racehorses.

Jim Beattie imported his stallions from England. He had three farms: a dairy farm in Warwick, a horse farm in Coventry, and a farm where he kept his stallions and breeding stock in Moosup, Connecticut, just over the state line. I became acquainted with the Beattie operation while I was still working for the federal government. When I first went into practice for myself, he asked me if I'd like to be his veterinarian and I gladly accepted. He became one of my principal clients. I visited his three farms on a regular basis. His imported stallions produced some of the finest racehorses in New England.

Meanwhile, I had become friends with George Wynhof, a Florida businessman who ran a string of racehorses at Narragansett Park in Pawtucket. We were introduced when I was recommended to take care of one of his horses after it had been shipped from Florida. After that, he visited my farm and I told him that eventually I wanted to get into breeding. He told me about a mare he had in Florida. He really wasn't interested in breeding horses, but this mare had been an especially good race mare for him. He said, "I'll give you this mare, if you're interested, and what I want is to be your partner, 50-50, when she produces her first foal."

I wanted to see the mare, so I flew to his farm outside of

Miami. He wanted me to pick out what I considered to be the best looking mare out of about fifty mares in the bunch. "If you pick three mares," he said, "my mare will be one of them," and sure enough, I picked out three mares and this mare was one of them.

She was beautiful. Her name was Scherzo, which on a page of music means *faster*. I brought her home and bred her to a stallion. She had a very nice foal, her first, which George named Dr. McQuatch. Dr. McQuatch won the first time we ran him and paid a huge amount of money. George was very happy, and Scherzo became the foundation mare for all my horses that came afterwards.

Now, back to Jim Beattie. After Scherzo had Dr. McQuatch, I wanted to breed her again. A mare caries a foal for eleven months; normally you breed a mare again a month after a foal is born. The objective is to have one foal a year, if you're lucky. That's normally the way it works. I was trying to decide who to breed Scherzo back to, when I was at Jim Beattie's farm at Moosup where he kept five stallions. There was one young stallion, Goodshot, that he had never used for breeding. The horse had come over from England and raced very successfully in this country until he injured himself and was retired to the farm. Beattie wasn't sure that he particularly liked this horse. He asked me who I was going to breed my mare to, and I said I hadn't decided.

"Why don't you breed your mare to one of my stallions?"

"Well, I'd like to, but how much are you going to charge me?"

He said that, because I was his vet, he would let me breed to any of his stallions without paying.

"Well then, I'd like to breed to Goodshot."

"Why do you want to breed to Goodshot? I'm not going to use him. I might even get rid of him."

"He's the best stallion you've got, Jim—his breeding, his race record, his conformation, everything about him."

"Well, if you like him so much, you breed to him."

And so I did, and the following year had a gorgeous colt, the only foal registered by Goodshot that year. I named him Mike Hudson, Jr., after my friend.

Scherzo and Mike Hudson, Jr., in the Kaplan pasture

Park Dandy

It was about 1962 when Jim Beattie's horse Park Dandy entered a $100,000 race at River Downs Track in Ohio. This was the first horse ever to leave New England to go to another state for a major stake race. It was quite a big story. The best horses in the country were there and Jim's horse was a long shot. The favorite was a horse owned by Allie Rubin, but we all bet varying sums of money on Park Dandy and we won! I remember flying home and celebrating on the plane. Beattie took over the whole plane, buying drinks for everybody and giving out $100 bills to the stewardesses. Jim's Irish trainer was Pat Brady. This was the crowning event in Brady's career and the biggest race that Beattie or anybody in this area had ever won.

The New England Futurity

Anyone who bred horses in New England aimed for the New England Futurity. The winner got $25,000, a huge sum of money at that time. The winners were usually the big breeders and the people with big farms.

I had only one mare and the foal named Mike Hudson, Jr. The New England Futurity was for two-year-olds, so when this horse became a two-year-old, I sent him to a new training center in Virginia built by Paul Mellon, one of the prominent people in United States racing. When Jim Beattie saw that Scherzo and Goodshot produced Mike Hudson, Jr., and realized what a beautiful horse he was, he decided to breed some of his mares to Goodshot.

After Mike Hudson, Jr., had been training a couple of months, the trainer at that stable, a Virginia horsewoman named Dorothy Lee, called me and asked, "Dr. Kaplan, who is your two-year-old by?"

"By Goodshot."

"Well, I don't know about his other foals, but this horse of yours looks like a good one. He's able to beat all these other horses that I have down here, and some of them are very high-priced horses of royal lineage."

As time went on, she became more and more enthusiastic, and when she shipped the horse back to me in the spring of 1960, I sent him on to Suffolk Downs in East Boston. We started him in a two-year-old race his first time out, and he won that race at a gallop by ten lengths. He won his second start, then his third. The fourth would be the New England Futurity.

At this point, I was still Jim Beattie's veterinarian, and he was still wishing me well, but he kept asking me if I was going to enter Mike Hudson, Jr., in the Futurity.

"I'm hoping to."

"You know, I'm going to run six horses in that Futurity by my other stallions. I wish you well."

But I could see that this was his own blood, his own stallion, and I knew if I beat his horses in the Futurity, it was going to be the end of our relationship.

Jim was sixty years old or better, but still a rough, tough former English-Irish football player whose language would embarrass a barroom sailor. At the races leading up to the Futurity, Jim's nephew Billy McGill would call and tell me, "Doc, you better watch out for Jim. If you win that Futurity, he's going to explode." Billy was my go-between, my conduit, for everything that was going on with Jim Beattie.

The day of the New England Futurity came, and with my family I arrived at Salem, New Hampshire along with Martha Watson and some neighborhood boys who had never been off their farms.

Sixteen horses had been entered. Ordinarily, a starting gate for horses holds twelve, but because of the four extra horses, an auxiliary gate had been installed. Jim Beattie had entered six two-year-olds, all by a stallion that he figured was the best he had, a horse named Castillian. Castillian had produced a lot of good runners, and Jim had reason to believe that he could overwhelm the opposition by entering six horses. (I don't believe that, in American racing history, one owner has ever entered six horses in one stake race. That's probably one for *Guinness World Records*.)

Mike Hudson, Jr., broke from the gate in front and led all the way. Jim Beattie's horses were in a row behind him. It was futile; they couldn't catch the outstanding two-year-old that I had raised.

In the Winner's Circle, there were at least twenty people, including all kinds of dignitaries; you would have thought it was a major classic race like the Kentucky Derby. But Jim Beattie was nowhere to be seen. On the way home, my wife and I discussed how upset Jim must be, and sure enough, when I got home, there was a call from Billy McGill.

"Doc, I've never seen Jim so infuriated. He's been calling you all kinds of names, that he never should have let you breed your mare to his stallion. He said you're due at the dairy farm on

(Above) Heading for the finish line at the New England Futurity, Mike Hudson, Jr. leads the way. (Below) The crowd of Kaplan family and friends enjoy this wonderful victory.

Tuesday." That was when I made my weekly rounds to examine the cows, checking for any problems that might have occurred during the week.

I arrived on the Tuesday and started to do my work. I was in the middle of a pregnancy examination, wearing a plastic sleeve and working through the cow's rectum, when Jim Beattie and Billy McGill walked into the barn.

Jim was a brawler; he was noted for starting fights in bar-rooms where he'd buy everybody a drink and then call somebody a name and start pushing. The next thing you knew, the stools were flying and the bottles were going. I knew his reputation. So, when he walked in with Billy, I thought, "Here it comes."

Jim walked up to me and said, "So, you think you're pretty

damn smart, don't you, beating me with my own blood? I knew I shouldn't have allowed you to breed to that stallion." Then he called me a particularly offensive name, at which point I withdrew my arm from the cow.

I took off the sleeve, "You're a poor sport yourself, aren't you, Jim?" and with that I backed away. I knew that I was the better fighter, but that he was capable doing something sneaky, like kicking me in the crotch or hitting me on the side my head. I was waiting for him to come at me, figuring I could handle him pretty easily.

At that point, Billy jumped in between us, "Come on, fellas." I walked away from what would have been an unfair fight. I picked up my equipment, put everything in my car, and went home. I told my wife, "Well, that's the end of working with Jim Beattie." He was my best account, but I had just won $25,000 and had a valuable horse and I was feeling pretty cocky.

"I'm all done with him. He's nobody I want to have anything to do with." The next morning, bright and early, before I left the house, Jim was at the door with Billy McGill. He put his hand out.

"Let bygones be bygones, Doc."

"No. I don't think so, Jim. I don't think I want to have anything to do with you and your farms, and you can find somebody else to do your work."

"Okay, do as you like," and off he went.

There were other attempts to get me to come back, but it never happened.

Lesson Learned

There are other stories I remember about Jim Beattie. One of the many lessons I learned as a young practitioner had occurred earlier at his dairy farm in Warwick. I was called one morning by Beattie's herdsman, Eddie Place. They had a nice, big Holstein heifer that was having difficulty calving. Most of the farmers in those days were pretty handy and could do a lot of things themselves. Eddie Place was capable, but he had tried and failed to deliver what turned out to be a huge calf from a first-time heifer. I arrived early in the morning, about five o'clock, just before they were to start milking. I had a very busy day ahead of me, a schedule that was going to keep me running probably until midnight, and I was hoping it was not going to be a long, drawn-out affair.

Two hours later, I decided that the only way I was going to deliver this calf was to do an embryotomy, which meant dissecting the calf and taking it out piece by piece. This was going to entail a half-day or most of the day. I felt that I shouldn't spend the whole day at it because I might ruin the cow and she wouldn't be any good for breeding. I rationalized everything, and I told Eddie that, all things considered, we ought to send this heifer to the butcher. And so I left.

A half hour or so later, Jim Beattie came in on his usual rounds, and asked what was happening. Eddie told him about my being there for two hours trying to deliver the calf, that I had advised sending the cow to the butcher. Jim said, "No such thing. That's a nice heifer and if he can't do it, maybe somebody else can."

They decided to call another veterinarian who had been around for a while. The man resented my steadily growing practice, which now included some of his former clients. So, he welcomed the opportunity to show me up when he was called. In essence, that's exactly what he did. He went there and worked a couple of hours and got the calf out. I was told about it the following day, that he did a good job and the heifer survived. I told myself that I'd learned a lesson that would last me the rest of my life: once you start a job, you finish it, one way or another. I have never forgotten that lesson I learned at Jim Beattie's barn.

Fun with the Farmers

Benjamin Carpenter

I remember so many stories about the dairy farmers. Benjamin Stanton Carpenter came from an old Yankee family of dairy farmers. Like his father before him, Ben had a dairy farm, his primary livelihood. He was also an entrepreneur. He sold potatoes at the house, he sold chickens, he had a little roadside stand. One of his other businesses was hauling junk, which he sold in Providence.

What amazed me was how many of these farmers were pretty sophisticated in a lot of ways, and that included investing in the stock market. Near the entrance of his barn, Ben had a big reproduction of *Whistler's Mother* and under it was a caption, "You mean that's all there is to it? Buy low, sell high?" In Ben's mind, that applied to all kinds of business. Ben used to repeat that caption, and I used to joke with him and hear him sing it in a singsong voice, "When I was a lad on my mother's knee, she used to sing a song to me. Buy low, sell high, buy low, sell high."

There were so many things that I learned from Ben; in his innate wisdom, he had some profound thoughts. Ben had some young heifers, maybe fourteen to eighteen months old, that he wanted to breed for the first time. He wanted me to examine eight of them. I went out there on the appointed day and examined the first heifer.

"Ben, this heifer's pregnant."

"Come on, Doc, don't kid with me. Nobody's pregnant. We don't have a bull. We bring a bull over from the other farm. We keep good records. That's impossible."

"Ben, this heifer is forty-five days pregnant."

"Well, all right," said he, figuring I was kidding him. "Let's do the others."

We lassoed the others, got them snugged up, examined them, and saw various problems, like cysts on ovaries. I gave an opinion on each one.

"Now, Doc, what about the big heifer?"

"She's pregnant."

"But Doc, that just can't be."

"Ben, do you want to bet ten dollars that she's pregnant?"

"You betcha." (Ben would only bet on a sure thing.) We shook hands on it.

With that, his son, Benny Jr., came in. When his father told him that the big heifer was pregnant, young Benny said, "She could be, Pa. Don't you remember you sold a heifer to Jim Card when she was a calf, and he had her artificially bred and then you bought her back? That's the one you bought back."

Well, Ben looked at me and took off his cap and threw it on the ground, and said, "Doc, you got me that time."

"Ben, don't ever bet a man at his own game. A lot of things I don't know, but that's one game I do know. When I say a cow's pregnant, she's pregnant." Ben was an honorable man. He reached in his pocket and gave me the ten dollars.

When I got home that night, I told my wife and we got a big kick out of it. I was watching the news later on and decided to have a little fun with Ben, who'd had his share of fun with me, but not that day. I knew he usually went to bed by nine o'clock, but his wife stayed up and sewed and read the Bible. She was not an early-to-bed person. I called his house and asked his wife to wake him up. He came to the phone, and I said, "Ben, this is Dr. Kaplan. Listen, you weren't watching the eleven o'clock news, were you? I just thought you'd be interested to know they had a story that a young veterinarian in South County beat Ben Carpenter for ten dollars." Well, he actually slammed the phone down, because he knew I was going to spread that story. But he had a good sense of humor and we joked about it years later. Ben said that's the first and last time anybody got him on something like that.

Wanton Carpenter

One day, home from my calls, I heard from Ben's brother Wanton. "Wanny" was one of half a dozen Carpenter boys, all farmers and entrepreneurs. Wanny, like his brother, had a big junk business and wanted to expand by buying a much bigger truck so he could take more scrap to the city. When he went to the bank to borrow $10,000 to buy the truck, the loan officer, Mr. Carpenter (no relation) said that Wanny would need to have a co-signer. So, Wanny said to me, "I thought of you. I wonder if you'd do me a favor and co-sign this note?"

Well, I had learned a long time ago that if you're thinking of co-signing for somebody and you're not willing to give him the money, you'd better not co-sign, because you're going to end up being the one to pay for it. I told Wanny to go back to the bank and tell Mr. Carpenter that I would be willing to lend him $15,000 if *he'll* co-sign.

"Gee, do you think he'll do that?"

"Well, if he wants me to do it, why wouldn't he do it?"

"I'll go down and ask him."

Pretty soon he came back and told me, "Mr. Carpenter says that you're in the veterinary business and he's in the banking business. He never heard of such a ridiculous idea."

"Well, I'm sorry, Wanny. If he's not willing to co-sign, then why should I?"

Clarence Wheeler

Clarence Wheeler had a nice barn, good cows, and good horses. He had a very large herd of milking Ayrshires, and he also had a bunch of horses, which he bought and sold at auctions. One day, a cow had just calved and then come down with milk fever. Clarence called me and I went right over. The cow was flat on the ground. I inserted a needle in the jugular vein and started infusing a calcium–magnesium–dextrose combination. I wanted to run the fluid in very slowly, and I had warmed it in a bucket of hot water before inserting the needle.

Some young boys, about fourteen or sixteen years old, were there, so I enlisted their help. I asked one boy, Nubby, to hold up the bottle of fluid, and another to lie across the cow's head to try to keep her from getting up too soon. I was on the floor. After ten minutes, I looked up to see how much of the bottle was left and I saw that hardly any had gone into the cow. It looked as if something was wrong.

I checked and finally realized that Nubby, a real cut-up, was pinching the tube so that the fluid wasn't moving. I caught him and said, "Hey, Nubby, you pinch that tube once more and you're going to be sorry." He was laughing and having a fine time. We finally got the fluid in.

While we were waiting for the cow to get up, I came up behind Nubby, tackled him, and threw him down in the hay. Then I hollered for the boys to come over. I said, "Watch this. I'm going to fix Nubby once and for all," and to Nubby, "I'm going to teach you a lesson." He was bawling and kicking and trying to get away. I had him pinned down. He started screaming, and he finally escaped.

As he ran to the house I heard, "I'll get even with you."

About a month later, I was back at the Wheeler barn to look at a horse with a problem. I parked my car where I usually did and took care of the horse and spent some time trading stories with Clarence. Then I went out to my car and turned the key. The whole front end exploded. The hood lifted up and I dived out to the side. I thought the end of the world was coming. I rolled away from the car expecting it to go up in flames, not knowing what had happened. I was terrified, and there, on top of the hill, was Nubby. He was laughing and hitting his legs and hollering, "I told you I'd get even with you."

Years later, I was at Jerry Titus's farm, and he said, "I was talking to an old friend of yours, and he wanted to be remembered to you. His name is Nubby. Do you remember him?"

"Remember him? I'll never forget him."

"Yeah. He told me he got even with you."

"I thought that was the end of the world."

Benny Filippi

The Filippis were a large family of horse enthusiasts. They owned a small farm just half a mile from mine. They had a particularly nice horse, a stallion, Iron Brand. When they retired Iron Brand to the farm, they decided they would stand him as a stud and they put one of the brothers, Benny, in charge. Now, Benny didn't know that much about horses. He thought he did, but he really didn't. He had prepared a nice stall for the stud, advertised him, and found a mare to breed to. The mare was in season and ready to be bred. Benny had somebody hold the mare and he brought the stallion out. As he recited the story to me, they tried to breed the mare for the next two hours, but without success.

Benny called me up and I said I'd see what I could do. I went around behind the mare and pulled her tail to the side. I saw that the mare's vulva had been sutured, sewn together, which is a common practice in racehorses, to keep the females from inhaling or sucking in air and dirt while they were racing, which can cause infection. Suturing the vulva made it impossible for the stallion to breed. It was very easy to resolve, but because Benny was a novice, he had no idea. I had to show him what the problem was.

"You see that, Benny? I could just about get my little finger in the bottom of the vulva. Mickey Mouse couldn't breed this mare."

"Yeah. I see what you mean. What are you going to do?"

"Well, I'm going to open her up. I'll put some anesthetic in there and undo the sutures so the stallion can penetrate her and get her pregnant."

My friend Leo Shurtleff owned a small dairy farm in West Kingston, about three miles away from Benny's. Leo tried to breed his first mares and had the same problem. I was away on a vacation, so he was stuck. Then he remembered that Benny Filippi had a stallion and figured that Benny would know what to do.

This is how Leo recounted the story to me. Benny walked

around behind the mare pulled the tail to the side, and said, "Come here, Leo. You see this?"

"Yeah. What's that?"

Benny said, "This mare is sutured and I don't think you're ever gonna breed a mare that's sutured. Mickey Mouse couldn't breed this mare."

Leo told me how embarrassed he was. "He made me feel like two cents, like I didn't know anything."

"Well, Leo, Benny Filippi is like a lot of experts I know. He's an expert by self-proclamation. He saw the same thing for the first time a month ago and now he's the expert and telling you that you're stupid."

Indian Wrestling

The younger farmers were very strong and physically fit, and I had a lot of fun with them. One of my favorite things was to challenge these rugged young men to Indian wrestle. Some of them knew the game. Some of them didn't. We'd go out and take our shirts off and wrestle. I had very strong wrists and fore-arms, and I knew a few tricks that would give me the advantage. I would always throw them quickly and they would come back for more, but it was never any contest. Some of the older, big-ger ones decided that they knew what I was doing and what my trick was, and they waited for me to come to the farm, saying, "We think we figured out what you do, the way you win these fights." Then I would beat them again. I developed a reputation around the farms as an expert Indian wrestler.

They wanted to try other games with me, but I would say, "No. Every man to his own game. I am a specialist in Indian wres-tling. I'm the champ, and you are going to have to beat me."

Burton Froberg was a big, rugged farmer, probably 240 or 250 pounds, and all muscle. He managed a herd of Ayrshire cows that were some of the best Ayrshires in the country. These cows were not only good milk producers, they also won at the national shows. Before Burt took over the farm, he was a star on the University of Rhode Island basketball team, which was the first in college basketball to regularly score 100 points in a game. Burt, however, had the arm of a baseball player. The routine was that when the other team scored a basket, Froberg would grab the ball and throw it the entire length of the court to the guy nearest the URI basket who would put the ball in the hoop. The team developed a national reputation under Coach Frank Keaney.

The only tournament at that time was the National Invitational Tournament (NIT). When URI went to Madison Square Garden, the entire town closed down. We'd fill a train; there would be extra cars. Others would drive carloads of people. Burt was on the team with Ernie Calvary, the one who shot the winning basket in the last few seconds of the game to win the NIT.

But Burt couldn't Indian wrestle. It drove him crazy that I not only threw him, but that I would insist we wrestle near the gutter where the cows did their cow flops. The loser was taking a chance of being thrown in the gutter, which would make him try all the harder. Burt would always say, "You know, there's gotta be something to it."

Later, at the farm, he took me aside, "Listen, I've been betting with Leo. We're betting on the sex of the new calf and whoever loses has to buy the other one a sundae. Right now, Leo is on a winning streak, and I owe him a bunch of sundaes. When Leo comes in, would you challenge me to Indian wrestling again and let me beat you so I can get even with Leo?"

"Okay, Burt. I'll do it."

When Leo came up, I asked, "Hey, Leo, do you want to Indian wrestle?"

"No, I'm not interested in Indian wrestling with you."

Then I asked Burt if he wanted to take me on.

Burt said, "I'm gonna beat you. I know your tricks and I'm going to beat you."

Leo bit, "You wanna bet six sundaes that you can't?"

So they bet six sundaes. We put on a big performance, pushing and grunting back and forth, and, finally, Burt threw me off

balance. Leo had a look on his face that said, "I can't believe it."
I think I let him down.

Charlie Cashman

Charlie Cashman had a big farm in Matunuck, down near the
salt water. In the old days, they used to take the horses and
wagons to the beach and collect seaweed, which was in abun-
dant supply and made an excellent fertilizer—an old Indian
trick. This was all Indian country before the Yankees got here.
They used dead fish and seaweed to fertilize their cornfields and
their land.

Charlie never used "vetinaries," as he called them, but he
started to use me when he found that I could save him money.
He had decided that, better than lose a cow, he would pay me,
and that is how he became a good client. After I did anything
at Charlie's barn, he made the same statement, "come to the
house," every time. He would not pay me in the barn or in front
of anybody, not even Lloyd. Charlie would sit down at his old
rolltop desk and take out a big leather purse with two big brass

Seaweed gatherers thought to be at the northern end of Scarborough Beach (courtesy of
the Pettaquamscutt Historical Society)

snaps on it. I used to tell Lloyd that when Charlie got ready to pay me, I could see his hands start to shake, but he would always pay me, and like all the farmers that I worked with, I was never stuck for a bill.

One day, when Charlie opened his big rolltop desk to pay me, I noticed some stock certificates, and I said, "Charlie, I didn't know you were interested in the stock market."

"Oh, yes. I've been in the stock market a long time."

"Really? What kind of stocks do you buy?"

"Oh, a stock broker once told me to buy the three G's: General Motors, General Electric, and General Tire. I've been buying them whenever I have some extra money."

I imagine that by the time Charlie died, he had acquired quite a few.

Once when I got to the farm, Charlie was sitting on a three-legged stool, milking a cow known as "Kicker." He had chains on the cow's hind legs and a rope over her back to restrain her. Even so, he was still having difficulty staying on the stool.

As I watched Charlie, I walked over to the other side of the barn and said to Lloyd, "That cow is like the rodeo. She's going to hurt Charlie."

"Oh, you know what happened to him; don't you?"

Charlie and Lester Browning are always trading cows. Charlie had a fresh Holstein, meaning she had just calved and gives the most milk. Charlie told Lester he had too much milk and he'd trade this nice fresh cow for something else, and Lester said he had a nice brown cow that he would trade for the Holstein. But there was one problem with her: when she calved she had a beautiful udder and gave a lot of milk, but within two weeks of calving, she would just dry up. The trade was consummated: a cow that didn't give any milk for a cow that kicked like the very devil. That was typical of those days. If Lester would ask Charlie, "How's that cow doin' that I traded you?" Charlie would say, "Best milkin' cow in the herd. Giving more milk than anybody. How's that other cow that I traded you?"

"That's a great cow. Good trade."

You never conceded that the other fellow got the better of you.

Lloyd Whitford

Charlie Cashman was an honorable man and widely respected. His daughter Louise was married to a fellow named Lloyd Whitford. Lloyd was enterprising and educated, a new breed of farmer who had lots of good ideas that were difficult to get across to people like Charlie, who believed in the old ways.

Lloyd, being progressive, kept asking his father-in-law Charlie about building a new barn. Finally, old Charlie gave in, and with a lot of local help and labor, they put up a beautiful big barn. Many people were involved, so on the first day the barn was to be used, we all gathered to see the cows go in; it was quite a ceremony. One on-looker was a German man, Count Oppersdorf. Everybody referred to him as the "Count." He was a connoisseur of everything. No matter what it was, he knew something about it. If Lloyd had a fine gun and could hit a

Lloyd Whitford's house

bull's-eye from 100 yards, the Count would say, "Very fine gun, but back in Germany, we have . . ." No matter what, it was a big joke.

One day, we were talking about binoculars and the Count said, "Well, American binoculars are good, but back in Germany, . . ." and one old fellow piped up, "Count, if everything's so good in Germany, how come you don't go back there?" That brought the house down, the Count included. He admitted they had him on that one.

There we were, all gathered at the barn to see the first cow go in. She jumped across the gutter, put her head in the stanchion, and then proceeded to have a bowel movement, which landed right in the gutter where it was supposed to. The Count jumped up and hollered, "Bull's-eye!" I still laugh about it, thinking about the way he punctuated the air with his finger with such glee.

Artificial Insemination in Dairy Cattle

Not only was I accepted by the farmers of the community, I also provided services they had never had, including taking care of sterility problems in cattle. When I arrived here, in order to get a dairy cow pregnant, a farmer would use a natural service, which meant he had to have his own bull. Later, some entrepreneurs came along and offered different breeds of bulls to the farmers to service their cows.

A cow's gestation period is nine months and ten to fourteen days. The objective was to have her calve at least every twelve months because, as the pregnancy progressed, the cow's milk production diminished. In order to renew the production of milk, a cow had to be pregnant and have a calf. At that time, a cow that produced twenty quarts of milk a day was considered a good one. Maybe twenty years later, through selective breeding and the upgrading of stock, it was not uncommon for a cow to produce 100 pounds, or fifty quarts, of milk a day. The high-producing Holstein-Friesians, the big black and white cows, were the most popular because they were the heaviest producers.

Many years later, artificial insemination opened up a whole new avenue for breeding cattle, and the University of Rhode Island was in at the beginning (it was the second university in the country to have such a program) and asked me to participate. The dean of the School of Agriculture was authorized to acquire a bull, and, after an exhaustive study, bought the first one, a Guernsey.

On the day that the bull arrived, there was a ceremony; a large crowd of university people, local farmers, and anyone interested in the program was invited, and the bull was paraded around. One young man, a student, piped up, "Doesn't a bull have two testicles?"

The dean said, "Of course."

"Well, I see only one."

Brushing the student aside, the dean went over to get a closer look. Sure enough, the bull had only one testicle. What an embarrassment. It was a source of great mirth, but it was all part of the process.

It wasn't long before URI had bulls representing every breed, and the process of reproduction through artificial insemination became a widely used method of dairy cow production. The plan was to keep bulls of various breeds; when a bull served a cow, an artificial vagina was used to catch the semen. Then the semen was divided and frozen into ampules—many ampules of semen could be produced from one service of a bull. Because the University of Rhode Island was in the forefront, and, of course, needed a veterinarian, I was in on the ground floor.

The dairy barn at the college (Special Collections Library, University of Rhode Island, used with permission)

George Causey

Bayfield Farm was established by George Causey. A Holstein farm, it became known throughout the entire United States and even Europe because of a bull named Ivanhoe that he co-owned with Aldo Panciera. Ivanhoe became the progenitor of many cows that made world records in milk production. I enjoyed a very nice relationship with George Causey, who also employed a well-known sterility expert, a Dr. Haubrick, who came from New Hampshire.

It was important that the cows calved every year. The offspring not only replenished the herd but went to many of the

Governor John O. Pastore awards trophy to Aldo Panciera, owner of Yearling Blue Ribbon Winner and Grand Champion at the 1949 state fair (courtesy of the Pettaquamscutt Historical Society)

big sales. One ejaculate from Ivanhoe would make forty or fifty ampules that could be frozen and stored and still be viable. It's amazing that, over fifty years later, semen from that bull Ivanhoe still shows up occasionally at sales and commands a very high price. (It is said that one ampule of Ivanhoe's frozen semen is worth $10,000.)

Dr. Haubrick traveled to Bayfield Farm regularly and was paid what seemed to me a huge fee. People in this area were willing to pay for him, because if they had any trouble getting a cow pregnant, they thought he was the man to find out what the problem was. George Causey had a world record cow. I think she was the dam of Ivanhoe, and she was having trouble getting pregnant. Dr. Haubrick had seen her and left a list of instructions for us to follow. The cow had been bred a few weeks before Dr. Haubrick's arrival at the farm, and, after examining the cow, he said that she was not pregnant, that she needed some hormones to get her to ovulate, which might help her get pregnant.

Harold Deering was the herdsman at Bayfield Farm. He and I became pretty good friends, so he asked me, "Doc, I wonder if you would consider doing me a favor? Dr. Haubrick said that this cow is not pregnant, but I believe she is. George is away. Could you examine this cow and, just between us, tell me what you find?"

Within a few moments, I told Harold, "This cow's pregnant."

"When George gets back, I'm going to tell him what we did, whether he likes it or not."

At this point, I was confident in my ability to do sterility work on cows. Dr. Haubrick was a famous breeding expert, but I felt that I was right. When George returned, he called Dr. Haubrick, who came back and re-examined the cow. "Yes," he said, "she is pregnant."

Well, that was a feather in my cap, and I felt pretty good about it.

A few weeks later, at five o'clock in the morning, we were at the Causey barn. George was concerned about a cow that was exhibiting symptoms of what turned out to be acute ketosis, which is essentially a lowering of the blood sugar. I told him how I felt about his use of Dr. Haubrick. "You pay him $100 to come down from New Hampshire, and you call me here early in the morning to look at a cow with a serious problem and I get just $15. If you think I'm not capable of doing your sterility work and you want to use Dr. Haubrick, you can call him the next time you have an emergency at five in the morning."

Earl Whitford

Earl Whitford was a good dairy farmer, but very, very careful with his money, a necessity for survival for most of the farmers. He didn't believe in spending money for a doctor. If he could use some old remedies that he had faith in, he would. So, he seldom used "vetinaries." Earl's family is still in Exeter, not far from here. One day Earl called me and said that one of his best cows had just had a calf, and the cow wasn't eating and had lost a lot of weight. He wanted me to come over and look at her. The cow obviously had lost a lot of weight. She wasn't eating, wasn't giving any milk, and when I listened to her heart and lungs, she gave a very characteristic ping sound.

Even today, this disease is still referred to as "hardware disease." A cow grazing in a pasture can pick up metal, like old staples or nails. Normally, the metal gets into the first stomach, the rumen, and eventually finds its way into the second stomach, the tripe or reticulum, where the diaphragm is located. If the nail penetrates the honeycomb, or the tripe, and gets into the thoracic cavity, which includes the heart and lungs, it can become a major problem, setting up a peritonitis.

In those days the only way you could remove metal was to do a surgical procedure called a rumenotomy. (Today, it is possible to insert a very powerful magnet into the rumen; the magnet is heavy enough to remain in the rumen for the remainder of the animal's life, and it can catch an amazing amount of metal and keep it there.) The rumenotomy was really quite a simple procedure involving an incision. Educated veterinarians were doing this routinely; it was a valid and effective procedure. I had done a number of them but felt I could stand a little more experience.

I told Earl that the cow had ingested a wire or nail or maybe even a bunch of them and that the metal had to be removed through surgery.

"What's this going to cost me?" Earl asked.

"It's going to cost $50."

"Will you guarantee it?"

"No, Earl, I don't guarantee. The only thing I guarantee in life is death and taxes and if you are going to want to go ahead with it, there's something you can do and it would save us a lot of time." I explained, "Between the last rib and the point of the hip, there is a large area where I'm going to make the incision; it has to be shaved and then coated with iodine two or three times so that the field is sterile." I drew an outline on the area.

Later that day, Earl called and said that he figured the surgery would be worth it. I told him I would do it that night if he was willing, at about nine o'clock. He said he would take care of the preparations for me. I arrived with all my equipment, which I had boiled, because that was the method of sterilization. (I got my sterilizers later, but boiling was the way to do it then. I would carry all the equipment in the same container that I had boiled it in, so all my instruments were sterilized and I was prepared for surgery.)

There must have been ten farmers in that barn, sitting on bales of hay. They had all come to see this new veterinarian perform the operation. I hadn't expected that and I started getting a little nervous. I knew that if I didn't find anything I would be in big trouble. With all those spectators, most of whom I knew, I started to panic. Now my heart was pounding, and I said to myself, "I hope this cow's got some wire. I'm either going to be a hero or I'm going the other way."

As I got ready to pick up my scalpel, Earl winked at the other farmers and said, "Now, Doc, you guarantee this, right?"

"Win or lose, it's going to cost you $50, Earl."

Luckily, I found a whole handful of nails, staples, and screws. I was a hero on that occasion. I demonstrated how to use new, modern veterinary and surgical techniques in a barn setting. I

did many rumenotomies after that and developed a pretty sat-
isfactory and rapid technique. We could do it routinely, because
hardware disease was a common malady.

Spud Mac's Steer

This story really belongs to Dr. Bob Conrad who arrived on the scene at South County Hospital. In the mid-1940s, when I came to Rhode Island, there were no medical specialties, like surgery or nephrology. General practitioners did it all. There was an obstetrics section, to handle births. By today's standards, it was a pretty primitive place. But with the advent of Dr. Conrad, the practice of medicine here began to change, and for the better. I was recently reminded of this story and all its variations, so I decided to visit Dr. Conrad to confirm the details.

Like other professionals in town at the time, Dr. Conrad maintained farm animals; he had sheep and pigs. If one of his animals needed to be slaughtered, he would take it to Spud Mac, a farmer and client of mine.

On one occasion, when Dr. Conrad and his young daughter Casey were at Spud Mac's, Spud expressed concern about one of his steers. It was thin, wasn't eating, had a hump back, and was grinding its teeth; it was common for cattle to pick up nails and wire while grazing and Spud wanted to know if Dr. Conrad could take an X-ray of the animal's stomach. (Today a machine could probably be capable of imaging in such a case, but in those days we didn't have anything like that.)

Dr. Conrad acquiesed, but he said Spud would have to take the animal to the hospital while he was on duty and preferably when no one else was around. And so they arranged a time. Spud trucked the steer to the hospital parking lot, and Dr. Conrad wheeled out a portable X-ray machine. They could see nothing on such a small machine, so Dr. Conrad suggested that they lead the animal inside, to the big X-ray machine. They managed to get the steer in the door before he balked. His footing failed him; he could gain no purchase on the linoleum flooring, and he stiffened up, all four legs splayed in all four directions. As they pulled him along the corridor, he proceeded to deposit cow flops all along the way. They did manage to find someone to clean up, and they did get the steer into the X-ray room. They tried and tried to get a result, but they couldn't. To no avail. An exercise in futility.

Unusual Practices

Penicillin

We have so many drugs today, I wonder how we treated anything or got an animal well with what we had back then—although we thought we were pretty modern compared to the old horse doctors. Back then, we had only the sulfa drugs, but during World War II penicillin became widely available. It was a wonder drug, not only in human but also in animal medicine. Conditions that had never responded to treatment, like certain streptococcal diseases affecting a cow's udder, were major problems; sud-

Fiftieth reunion at Penn (Doc front row, right)

denly they became easy to treat. Penicillin cleared things right up and it was relatively cheap. So suddenly, we were miracle workers with this treatment.

At that time, my younger brother Morey was in Italy with the Army. The family sent him packages of various things, socks and goodies of all kinds, whatever we thought he might like. He wrote me a letter telling me that he really appreciated the packages, but he could get anything he needed cheaper at the PX. Instead, he would like me to send him some penicillin, normally available only to veterinarians or medical doctors. He said that syphilis was a big problem in Italy. A lot of people, even the gentry, had the disease. Penicillin was in short supply and was literally priceless. If I sent some penicillin, he could get friends to trade it on the black market.

I sent him the penicillin, and within a few weeks, I received pictures of Morey and his buddies in a Roman villa and a letter that they were living like the old Roman rulers. They had their own servants, automobile, chauffeurs, and everything else. And he reported, "We've got to spend the money that we're making because they're paying us in *lire*." Later, Morey told his kids, "We lived like kings. We had everything, all because of the penicillin that your uncle sent me."

KY Jelly

At my fiftieth vet school reunion, fifteen or more of my classmates gathered at our banquet, and we were all called upon to say a few words. I talked about what I was doing, still practicing, working on wild horses. Everybody else had been retired for quite a while. Afterwards, we had an informal gathering, and different classmates told more stories, so I did too. This one brought the house down.

Way back, early in my practice, I noticed in one of the journals a big advertisement for a new product, a lubricant called KY Jelly, which is still popular and has many different uses. When the product was still new, the manufacturer offered some nice prizes for the best suggestions, in fifty words or less, for new uses for KY Jelly, including a trip to the Caribbean, a stereo set, equipment, and fifty smaller prizes. In my entry, I said I found KY Jelly to be an excellent lubricant. I had also found it be very useful when I was in the bedroom with my wife and did not want to be disturbed by the children. I would smear some KY Jelly on the doorknobs. Sure enough, I won a prize, a year's supply of KY Jelly.

Practicing Human Medicine Without a License

This story involves a friend of mine, whose name I won't use, for reasons that will become obvious. He came to my office one night and asked if he could speak to me privately. He said he had a fight with his wife the previous night, left the house, went to a bar, and got drunk. When he woke up he was in a strange room, in a strange bed, with a strange woman. "Believe me, this woman didn't look too savory. I'm scared to death that I caught something from her. Can you give me a shot of penicillin?"

Now, he was a good friend. I knew him well enough, but this was beyond the regular practice of veterinary medicine. So, I said, "Okay, drop your pants. I'm gonna give it to you in your rear end." I loaded the syringe with the proper human dosage, attached the largest size horse needle I had, and I gave him the shot.

He jumped, hollering and grabbing his rear end, "What in the world was that needle you gave me?"

I held it up, and said, "It's a fourteen gauge. It's the biggest needle made, and the reason I gave it to you is that I want you to remember it, so that it won't ever happen again."

He went out of here rubbing his backside, saying, "Believe me, I got the point."

The Old-fashioned Ways

Henry Kenyon was a dairy farmer with a very large family—over ten children, a typical farm family. With baseball as the national pastime, a lot of them played in the farmers' league and many families were big enough to make up a team, like the Briggs family, who all were great baseball players. A daughter, Wilma Briggs, even ended up in the women's professional league that they called "a league of their own." She was a catcher, as I remember.

My wife knew my schedule and all the routes among the farms. People knew to get in touch with me through her, because she would monitor the telephone at the office and have a general idea of where I was at any time. That way, I wouldn't need to backtrack if I was already in the area when a call came in. She would call the farm and leave a message.

So, when I got to the Kenyon Farm one day, Henry was waiting on the steps of the farmhouse. "Doctor, before you take care of my cows, Lester Tefft has a steer that's down. He called your house and your wife told him you were on your way here." Lester lived close by. These farmers were their own doctors; they seldom needed a veterinarian and when they did call, it was serious. Henry told me that Lester was waiting for me to call him back.

"Okay, Henry, would you call Lester and tell him I can't get over there, but if he'll call a friend of mine over in Hope Valley, Father Bernard, a Catholic priest, he'll go over there and give that steer the last rites."

"Come on, Doc, stop the kidding."

"Henry, I'm not kidding. I'm serious. I'm not going over there, because the steer is probably within a half hour of dying. It will be an exercise in futility. He'll take up my time and it'll cost Lester money."

A couple of weeks later when I was at the farm, Henry said, "Hey, Doc, you will be interested to know that Lester's steer died about fifteen minutes after he called here."

We had many farmers' banquets, and various members of the clergy would give the benediction. Young Father Bernard was there one time, and I asked him, "Father, did you ever get a call from someone about giving an animal the last rites?"

"No, why would I?"

So I told him the story. "Now, you are my ace in the hole. When I want to get out of something and I know an animal is going to die, I'm going to tell the farmer to call you."

He had a good sense of humor. "Sure," he said, "You do that."

I'd heard from a number of people that an old friend had died. Originally from Oklahoma, he was a farmer here. He had all kinds of animals. He and his boys started a construction business as a sideline. When I asked what happened to him, I was told that he hadn't been in the best of health and that he and the boys had been at a truck pull, their favorite sport (a more modern version of the horse pulls at the country fairs). My friend had a heart attack there and died very quickly.

They called the rescue squad, but there was nothing to be done and I heard that there was quite a ruckus. The three boys wanted to put their father in the pickup and take him home.

Horse-pulling the old-fashioned way (courtesy of the Pettaquamscutt Historical Society)

They insisted that was the way to do it. There was a great deal of discussion, as the others were much against that idea. Somebody called the funeral director, who persuaded the boys not to put their father in the pickup truck to take him home. To the boys, it was just the most natural thing to do. They didn't think twice about it. That was how they were raised. It might sound amusing now, but back in the old days that was common-sense thinking.

Rooster Fights

In a chicken yard, roosters will fight; they will act like a couple of kids wrestling in a schoolyard. The dominant bird wins the fight and the other one ruffles his feathers, so no animal really gets hurt. What I didn't realize is that when you put iron spurs on the same animals to fight, they can kill each other. First they would be trained to fight without spurs, and then the spurs would be put on.

I hadn't known anything about rooster fights until one of the farmers told me about them. "You know, they bet some really big money on those fights. People come from all over. There's a group from Long Island that is stimulating their chickens with something. I'd like to know what it is." I said, "Well, I wouldn't know anything about that, but there are a lot of stimulants that could be used." If a large animal had low blood pressure or an impairment in heart function or breathing, we had stimulants to give it, along with the other drugs we use. This farmer wanted to try something on the roosters, just to see. I told him to come over sometime with a couple, and we'd put them in the big stallion stall and let them have a little fight and see what happened. I never thought anything would come of it.

But, one night, this farmer came into the driveway. "Doc, we got a couple of crates of roosters here. Can you come down to the barn?"

I went in and told my wife that the farmer had a couple of sick calves down at the stable. She never knew any of this; she would have been horrified. Despite my misgivings, I went along to the barn.

They first brought out two chickens, a young chicken they thought quite a bit of and an older chicken that had lost its will to fight, but hadn't yet gotten killed in a fight. They had saved him, I guess, for breeding. They put the two chickens down in the stall. They didn't have any spurs on and they started to fight. The younger chicken kept knocking the old chicken down and jumping on him. The old chicken didn't want to fight. No contest. After we saw that, the farmer said, "Now, Doc, give the old chicken something and see if it makes him want to fight." I had no idea what dosage to give a chicken. I'd have to have a tuberculin needle to measure out such a small quantity. I had a drug that was popular then, Ritalin, and I measured out a fraction in the syringe. I didn't know where to give a chicken an injection, but I figured I'd give it to him under the skin.

When chickens are going to fight in the ring, the owners allow them to peck at each other to get them into a fighting mood. They did that but the old chicken still didn't want to fight, so they said, "How long should we wait?" We waited five minutes and put the two chickens down. The young chicken jumped on top of the old one and beat him up again. I said, "I'm not going to stay down here all night and fool around with these chickens." We stood around a little while longer.

All of a sudden, the old chicken started crowing and pecking at the other chicken and acting as if he wanted to fight. They said, "Look at that, he wants to fight." So, they put the two chickens down, and sure enough, that old chicken jumped on the young one and started beating up on him. Everyone was cheering. When it was all finished, they said, "We knew those guys from Long Island were using something."

Of course, I didn't tell them what the drug was.

Funny, when I think of it now, I had noticed at the Whitford farm that there were a lot of beautiful roosters, big, red roosters with long spikes on their legs, all kept in individual pens. I had never seen roosters with such gorgeous plumage. "What do you raise the chickens for, Earl?"

"Just for the sport of it. We put them outside and let them

tangle around and fight each other. They don't hurt each other, but when they fight the real chickens with the spikes on their legs, they can kill each other. It's a blood sport."

That seemed kind of strange, but I didn't give it much thought.

I began to notice that this was a hobby of the younger farmers. The older farmers were not into it. One day, I was over at the Casey farm, a historical farm in North Kingstown overlooking Narragansett Bay. This gorgeous 300-acre property was left by an old sea captain and is now managed by Historic New England. Today it is open for visitors and is still a beautiful working farm. At that time, the resident manager was a colorful character named Archie Rose. Archie was a sportsman, a man-about-town, and knew something about everything. He also boarded some of George P. Clark's fine Guernsey cattle from Horseshoe Falls in Shannock.

I noticed Archie had some roosters, and I said to him, "That's quite a hobby."

"Oh, yeah. It's quite a sport."

"What do you mean, 'sport,' Archie?"

Casey Farm

"Oh, don't you know about the chicken fights?"

"No, I've never seen one."

He told me that lots of guys around here were into fighting roosters. I asked where they did this, and he said, "We have a place in Ledyard, Connecticut. We have fights every week."

Ledyard is close to the Rhode Island line and is now the site of Foxwoods, the Indian casino that's the biggest in the United States and the most profitable. Back then it was a little rural town with small farms, frequented by only a few people, including some impoverished Indians.

Archie told me that people came from all over the country every weekend to fight their roosters and that a lot of money changed hands. He asked me if I'd like to go.

"Archie, are you kidding? First of all, it's illegal, and the idea of a veterinarian getting caught at such a fight is unthinkable."

"Do you know how long these chicken fights have been going on? Ten years. It's all taken care of with the local constable."

"Well, I don't want to take a chance."

A year later, I was still hearing about the rooster fights and curiosity got the better of me. I asked Archie, "When's the next one?"

"This coming week. A pretty good one."

"Well, I'd like to see what it's about."

"Okay, how do you want to arrange this?"

"Archie, you call my house tonight at seven o'clock, and I'll let my wife answer the phone. Tell her you have a cow in big trouble trying to calve, that she's thrown her uterus out, and it's going to be a long night."

The call came through, as planned. Archie and I drove to Ledyard, which took us about forty-five minutes. We went up a rural road and the first thing we came to was an iron gate with two guys standing there. They looked in the car and Archie said, "He's okay," so they raised the gate. Then we came to another gate with two more guards. Now we were in the woods about half a mile. Another quarter mile down the road, we got to a big, big two-storey chicken house, a legitimate-looking poultry farm. We went down a few steps to the basement, and there was a steel door. Archie vouched for me, and then he tapped on the door. The fellow inside unlocked that door for us.

I was absolutely astounded. There were refreshment stands, a bar, two rings with fights going on in each ring, and $100 bills on the floor. I couldn't believe that such a thing went on and that I never knew about it. I was such an innocent. I was amazed.

I couldn't wait to get out of there; I worried about getting caught, but I had to wait for Archie. I didn't bet and I was apprehensive the whole time. I saw all these farmer friends of mine. They all greeted me. Archie and I left about midnight.

My wife—we'd been married over fifty years then—was sitting up waiting for me, telling me how sorry she was that I had had such a long day. That was the clincher for me. As long as I was out on calls, she couldn't fall asleep.

A month later, I was at Archie Rose's farm again, and he asked if I wanted to go to another chicken fight.

"Archie, I've gone to my first and last chicken fight."

"But this is a good one and it's right close by, on Old Baptist Road in North Kingstown."

I pointed out to him that the State Police barracks were not a half a mile away on Route One. "I've gone to my first and last chicken fight, Archie," I repeated, "I don't want to see anymore."

The next morning, bright and early, as I was watching the local news on television, the first item was "State Police Raid Chicken Fights in North Kingstown." They caught so many people that I knew, including Archie and a lot of respectable farmers. They had to send for school buses to take them away. A lot of them pulled their coats up over their heads, as if they belonged to the Mafia. I sat there thinking, "Someone is looking after me." Imagine what would have happened to my career if I had been caught coming out of a chicken fight. A lot of my clients would have left me, and the rest of them would have been shaking their heads in disbelief. It taught me a good lesson, which I already knew, but that just reinforced it.

Faith Healing

E. Varror "Vera" Smith was a very nice, God-fearing, religious woman who was a member of the Maine family that established Maine's I Scream Parlor in Wakefield. It was the principal meeting place in town. The ice cream stand was directly across from two dairy farms, both of which are now shopping areas.

A big treat was to go to Peace Dale and have all the spaghetti and meatballs that you could eat for fifty cents, then go to the movies for a quarter, and afterwards have a ten-cent cone at Maine's. That made a very nice evening and that's what many of us did.

Vera was also quite the horsewoman. She had a very nice horse, which she kept across the street from me at the Sturges stable, where I was the veterinarian. One evening, Vera called to tell me that there was something wrong with her horse. The mare was rolling in the stall, apparently in agony. I went right over. She was having colic. There are various causes of colic, and very often it's fatal. We didn't have the drugs then that we have now; today we can treat colic in horses without surgery.

The horse was in distress. Her gums were pale, and her heartbeat was too rapid to count. Vera wondered, "Do you think you can do anything for her?"

"Well, I'm going to try, Vera."

After about an hour, Vera said she was going home and she gave me permission to do whatever I had to. I stayed up half the night with this horse, and I kept telling the young woman who was managing the stable that we were going to lose this one. The mare was rolling to one side and then the other, and then onto her back. I speculated that there was a twist in her intestine. Suddenly, she jumped to her feet and went over and started eating hay, a sign that the colic was over.

I stayed for another half hour or so, and the horse was obviously fine. She was shaking herself, drinking water, and eating hay. By this time, it was early in the morning. I called to give Vera the good news.

"I know," she said, "the mare's fine, right?"

"How did you know that, Vera?"

"I went home and called somebody in Providence and he's been working on her all night."

"Somebody in Providence has been working on her all night?"

"Oh, yes."

It turns out she was a Christian Scientist, and when I had given her the grim prognosis that I thought the horse was going to die, she went home and called someone in Providence who said he would pray for the horse. I was astonished, and I said to Vera, "Well, that's great, Vera, but I'm still going to send you a bill." She laughed and said, "Oh, I expected that." I could tell she was sure that my role in that episode was minimal. And who knows, maybe she was right.

Frank Nichols

Back in the 1960s, we didn't see too many cars in this area. I was surrounded by farms, dairy farms, behind me and beside me. A young man next door to me had a little milk house and milked about a dozen cows, and up the road was a fellow, Frank Nichols, with a small farm. Frank had married Della, a woman I would guess to be twenty-five years younger. The story goes that Frank discovered her in Exeter. Della was a farmer's daughter and a rugged six-footer whom he had observed working better than any man he ever saw. He persuaded Della to marry him.

They had some cows, raised vegetables, and ground out a living doing various other things. Frank came over here one Sunday (a lot of these things seem to happen on Sundays) and rang the doorbell. He said, "Doctor, I hate to bother you on a Sunday, but I want to talk to you about Della's cow. Della thinks that there is something wrong with her."

"What makes Della think there is something wrong?"

"Well, she was giving about twenty quarts of milk, and then a few days ago, she stopped eating and is giving hardly any milk. Her udder is a little hard. Just to satisfy Della, could you come over and look at her?"

He offered to take me over and bring me back. By doing that, he could pay me little or nothing instead of my having to make a special call. I knew Frank was pretty careful with his money, so I said, "No, Frank, a lot of stuff I might need is in the car. You go ahead, and I'll be right behind you."

As I pulled up to his barn, Frank was standing there with a huge squash in his hand. He said, "Doctor, did you ever in your life see a bigger, nicer squash than this one? Why don't you put this in your car and take it along. Your wife can cut that up and cook it, and you'll have enough squash to eat for a whole year."

"No thanks, Frank," I said. That was just another ruse to soften me up.

I went into the barn and the cow looked poor. She hung her head and was thin, and I said, "Frank, this cow doesn't look too good. How old is she?"

"Oh, she is just a young cow, second calf."

"Well, she looks pretty thin."

"I think they're better off that way. It's not good to feed them too good and get them fat."

"Well, yes. You've got something there, Frank." I examined the cow, and I said, "Well, Frank, she has ketosis."

"What do you do for that?"

"I have a new drug here that works very well, and I think you will find she will come along all right." I treated the cow and told Frank to let me know if she wasn't better in a couple of days, eating and starting to produce more milk. He paid me, and I went home and told my wife how good old Frank had tried to get the better of me.

It wasn't a couple of weeks later that I ran into the state veterinarian who was doing TB testing. He had just been to Frank's and stopped over to see me. "I just tested that cow you treated for Frank Nichols and he told me that she picked right up. What did you treat her for?"

"Ketosis."

"Well, when I asked Frank, he said, 'Something I never heard of . . . teethosis.' That's why I stopped over to see you, because that was a new one on me."

Anyhow, the cow got better and the joke went around for quite a while about this new disease known as "eating your own teeth."

Frank had a close friend, Colin Brown, who had a large dairy herd of excellent cows. They were friends since boyhood, and after they both married, the two couples would get together every once in a while. In order to save money, they would always use one car if they were going to a grange meeting or some other farmer function, their main form of entertainment. Once in a while, they would go as far as Newport. Whenever they went anywhere, they got separate checks because that way the one could not get the better of the other.

The two couples had always wanted to go to Florida. They had the road maps. They planned how they could get away, and of course, they were going to drive in one car. When the time finally came, they decided to go in Frank's car. They agreed that they would keep track and that they would take turns filling the gas tank. The idea was to get the other to pay more.

No sooner had they started on the trip when Frank's wife Della handed a little packet of chocolate buds to Colin and his wife and told them to help themselves. Frank piped up, "You know, it's a long way to Florida, we'll have to be buying some more. This package has got to last." He wasn't joking, and Della stopped passing the chocolates.

They agreed that they would stop for gas when the needle pointed exactly at one-quarter full. That worked until they got down to Miami. A day or two later, Frank said to Colin, "I'd like to go up and see Crystal Springs," which was a couple hundred miles away. So they drove to Crystal Springs and enjoyed their stay. On the way home, Frank told Colin that it was his turn to take care of the gas. Colin asked, "What do you mean? You invited us on this side trip. I didn't ask to go. It was your idea." Accusations flew back and forth. They were so mad at each other that they didn't speak all the way home or afterwards.

I heard this story from somebody else. So when I saw Frank, I said, "What's this I hear about you and Colin?" He told me how Colin tried to cheat him, that he couldn't trust him. And then I saw Colin and told him I had just come from Frank's. And Colin started in on Frank. It went on for a long time. I don't think they ever did make up. It was typical of those guys then.

Portuguese Wisdom

Aquidneck Island, believe it or not, was once an agrarian island. It included Middletown and Portsmouth to the north and Newport proper at its southern end. Back then, I would say three-quarters of that huge island was dairy farms. Today, there are only two or three dairy farms on the entire island. Everything has been developed as homes and hotels. It is just a beautiful place, particularly in the summer with the mansions and all the historic preservation.

In my time, it was inhabited mostly by Portuguese immigrants, who had settled on that fertile land and developed dairy farms. The Portuguese were excellent dairy farmers, and usually the whole family participated. Their care of cows was meticulous, none better. I was the only veterinarian over there for quite a while. As I got to know a lot of the farmers I would come home with Portuguese sweet bread, which was filled with all sorts of goodies. They knew I liked the bread, and always had a freshly baked loaf for me to take home. They made a ceremony out of it.

Anyhow, I walked into a barn over there one day and came upon a young boy and his grandfather. The young boy was holding his hand out and the grandfather was urinating on it. The grandfather said, "Hi, Doctor, be with you in a minute."

"What are you doing there?"

"Oh, my grandson has an infected hand. In the old country, this is how we take care of infection."

Apparently, it worked. Now there is a wonder drug called urea, manufactured from urine.

I castrated a horse in Newport for a young Portuguese farmer. I gave the animal a little sedative in the vein and then blocked his testicles with anesthetic and proceeded to remove them. All the while, the horse just stood there and didn't feel a thing, no pain. It went very smoothly. The man's immigrant father observed the whole thing and marveled at how nicely it was done, saying, "In the old country, they would take a horse and put him in a straight stall, and put a twitch on his nose and somebody would hold his tail over his back. Another man would go behind with two red bricks and bring the bricks together, crushing the testicles."

"Oh, my God. That must have hurt."

"Only when you got your thumb between the bricks," said the father.

My Run-ins with the Law

The Speeding Ticket

I inspected quite a few dairy farms on Aquidneck Island. Back then, in order to get there, I had to go over the Jamestown Bridge and then take the ferry across Narragansett Bay to Newport. The last ferry returning to Jamestown was at five-thirty in the afternoon. If I missed it, it would take me about three and a half hours to get home—up to Bristol, over through Providence, and then back down south. So, anytime I was there, I always made sure to catch that ferry.

One day, I was held up, and I knew I was going to have to speed to make the ferry. I was driving through Portsmouth, when the State Police waved me over. There was no question that I was exceeding the speed limit, but usually, I could talk myself out of a ticket. I would say that I was a veterinarian, which was obvious from all the things in my car, but this man was really arrogant.

"What's the charge, Officer? I know I was speeding, but I didn't think I was going that fast."

He growled, "Who do you think you are? A wise guy?" and he poked his finger in my chest.

Well, back in those days, I had a short fuse, and I could take care of myself in a fight. I said to him, "You're pretty brave in that uniform. If you want to go up that side road and lay your gun belt down and take off your coat, I'll show you something about poking somebody."

"Uh, well, you *are* a wise guy." He wrote me up and gave me the ticket.

Now I was going to miss the ferry. At that point, I was beside myself. I sped the rest of the way and didn't care what happened. I could see that the ferry hadn't left the dock yet and I started blowing my horn. They were just closing the gate when I pulled up. The crew on the ferry knew me, so they opened the gate and I made it after all.

This was early on in Kingston. I wasn't married at the time, and still staying at President Edwards' house. Mrs. Day lived there and made the rules (the one I remember most was that any tenant entertaining a guest of the opposite gender was required to keep the bedroom door open). About a week later, early in the morning before I left for work, Mrs. Day knocked on my door and said, "There's a state policeman here for you." It was my friend Gil Gallagher. He was standing there with a smile on his face.

"Boy," he said, "you picked a good one. Of all the State Police, you had to pick on that guy over in Portsmouth. He even gave my brother, Rags, a ticket." (Rags was also a state policeman.)

"He's absolutely the worst person we have on the force. The judge over there has issued an arrest warrant for you. You are charged with abusive language and threatening a state policeman. He gave you a ticket, didn't he?"

"Yes, he gave me a ticket, and I thought he would let me know about the hearing."

"It said right on the ticket when you were supposed to appear in court. You were supposed to appear in Newport three days ago. When I got the order to pick you up I said, 'What's the Doc done now?' I called Judge Sullivan in Newport and told him that there must be something wrong, that Dr. Kaplan is a veterinarian, and he's a friend of mine, and then I told him about this state policeman that was giving me all this trouble. So Sullivan told me to make sure you show up for court tomorrow, plead guilty, don't give him any flack, and he'll fine you thirty-five dollars."

I went over there, as instructed, and I stood before Judge

Sullivan, who was in his black robes, sitting behind one of those big, old-fashioned desks with the lamps at each end. He started reading the charges, and I thought, "Gee, that cop has charged me with everything in the book. I'm not going to sit still for this. I'll tell the judge about this guy, how he shouldn't be on the police force and all of that."

Then the judge looked down at me and said, "How do you plead?"

I opened my mouth to start in, and I remembered what Gil told me. "Guilty, Your Honor," and paid the thirty-five dollars. I've never had a ticket since.

A Moment of Truth

I have been stopped by the State Police at other times, usually on a call. One state policeman stopped me when I was exceeding the limit and I told him that I was Dr. Kaplan from Wakefield, on my way to an emergency, where a cow was trying to have a calf. He looked in my car and looked at my license, and I mentioned a few names, including Gil Gallagher, and he said, "Well, okay. Where is the farm?" I told him, and he said, "You know, I always wanted to see a cow have a calf. Go ahead, I'll follow you."

I thought, "Oh, my God. I'm just going over there to treat a few cows for foot rot or mastitis and here's this cruiser following me."

When I pulled in, the herdsman, Joe Cabral, came out. He saw the cruiser and I said, "Joe, where's that cow? Is it bad? Has she calved?"

Joe caught right on, "Yes, she has, and everything's all right."

The state policeman came along and asked to see the calf. They had a special barn for calvings, and there was a cow in there with a calf that was about two weeks old. Joe said, "There she is." The state policeman spent the next half hour looking at all the cows and calves. I don't think he would have given me a ticket even if he had found out the truth.

The IRS

Several newspaper stories have been written about my veterinary practice. It seemed that reporters would call me whenever they ran out of material and ask to join me on my rounds. On this particular day, a very good reporter named Bill Rodriguez called, wanting to do an article about a day in the life of a veterinarian. He had a little recorder with him and we talked in the car. In the course of the day, he got a lot of information for a story.

We were at a horse farm, and when we got done, Bill asked me how many horses I had in my practice. Then and now, nothing has changed: people exaggerate. If I ran into another vet, and if things were slow, or if he were starving, or if he didn't have any work and I asked him how things were going, he would say, "I'm going day and night, seven days a week." In other words, never admit that things are slow or how tough it is to make a living. You always exaggerate. And when we went back to school reunions, this was the game, to see who could throw the most bull, always telling how successful we were and never mentioning our failures.

Here is where I made my fatal mistake. In the entire state of Rhode Island, I would say that there were probably a hundred farms. But when Bill asked me how many farms I took care of, I said, "I don't know for sure, but I guess I must have five hundred farms and a couple thousand horses."

He published the story. It was a big story. I knew that any veterinarians who read it would know it was an exaggeration. A couple of weeks later, on a Wednesday, my day off, I was cutting the grass around home, and a car pulled up. Three people got out. One fellow came over and said, "Are you Dr. Kaplan?"

"Yes."

He flashed his gold badge. He said they were from the Internal Revenue. "We would like to talk with you."

I was shocked.

When I asked them what the problem was, they said, "Let's go into the house and talk." One of the agents said, "You don't have to answer these questions. If you want to get a lawyer or not, that is your privilege."

"I don't have anything to hide. I'll be glad to talk to you. What's this all about?"

He proceeded to ask me a whole bunch of questions. Did I have a boat? A vacation home? Stocks and bonds? Any businesses that I operated under another name? I answered all their questions straightforwardly and honestly.

He said, "Well, do you mind if we borrow your files? We'll bring them back in a couple of days."

"Sure." I had no qualms about that, and I started to get the files. I just stood there a minute and then I turned back and said, "Do you know? I can't imagine what this is all about. I'm not worried that I've done something, had some big income that I didn't report or whatever. So I'm not going to give you these files. I'm going to call a lawyer."

I called a prominent lawyer in Providence. When he asked me what it was all about, I told him that I didn't have a clue. And he said, "Now, I want you to tell me everything. I don't want any surprises."

"No, there isn't anything that I can think of. I've been very careful in reporting all my income. I have no hidden income."

"Well, why would they come down on you like this? If you can assure me that this is what you have in holdings, I don't think you have anything to worry about."

A year went by. I still hadn't heard from the IRS, so I asked my lawyer to find out if they were either going to clear me or take action. He reported that they had a backlog but in due time would let us know. Of course, this was a great mental burden for me, because I had never experienced anything like this.

Then one day I came home, and my wife had a big smile on her face. She was holding a letter from the IRS, a brief statement that they were pleased to inform me that there would be no further investigation. I was still puzzled about it all until one day, when I was in Saunderstown taking care of a couple of Tennessee walking horses for an elderly client. Afterwards, we chatted. This man was obviously very well educated, loved his animals and the farm. I asked him what kind of work he did before he retired.

"I was head of the IRS office in Providence." He told me how many years he had been there.

"Well you are just the man to ask." I told him about that story in the newspaper. "Do you think that's what triggered the whole thing?"

"You better believe it. We have people up there whose whole job is to read the newspapers and look for leads about people who are hiding income."

This whole business took a year out of my life and scared me to death. I learned my lesson: little white lies are okay, but not big lies. As the caller at the square dance said, "If you want to dance, you've got to pay the fiddler."

How I Won the Egg Laying Contest

The University of Rhode Island had a laying contest that was of great interest around here. The competition took place at the poultry farm at URI's East Farm. The farmers would bring ten or twelve of their best laying hens, which would then be put into individual chicken houses that were marked. In the past, some contestants were suspected of putting extra eggs in the chicken pens, to increase their score count. As a result, the doors were double-locked by one person who picked up the eggs morning and night and counted and recorded them. There was no monkey business with the chicken contest. At the end of every month, the winner was announced in the local newspaper.

The country fairs around here were real farmer fairs then. Now, they're commercial. To have a grand champion pen of laying hens was a great honor and a worthy goal. One fellow in particular seemed to win almost every time, and it was frustrating for the other competitors.

I was at the university one day talking to some of the people in the poultry department, when a young fellow showed me an article that concerned a new strain of chickens developed in Israel. They were white chickens, like Leghorns, but they

Contest rules (Special Collections Library, University of Rhode Island, used with permission)

were a cross-breed that had been developed to produce a super-laying chicken, good for laying eggs only. They laid so many eggs and converted their feed to eggs so quickly that they were very thin and rangy, but they were "laying fools" according to this fellow. The article gave the name of the director of the farm where these chickens had been developed.

I thought I'd have a little fun, so I wrote a letter asking if there was any possibility of getting some of these hens. The director wrote back to say he would be glad to send me some fertile eggs, which I could incubate. All I had to do was pay for the shipping and send the crates back to him. I received three dozen fertilized eggs. I bought a small incubator from Sears Roebuck, put it in my basement and started incubating the eggs.

They really were fertile eggs, yielding about thirty live chicks, which I raised. I ended up with maybe a dozen super-nice female chickens that started laying when they were less than a year old. They laid small eggs at that point; then, as they matured, they became beautiful birds and I couldn't keep enough feed in front of them.

Now I was ready to challenge the fellow who had been bragging about winning the chicken contest all the time. I went to East Farm and said I had a batch of chickens I wanted to enter in the laying contest. That started my long winning streak, and the headline in the local paper would read, "Kaplan Chickens Win for Fourth Straight Month." I was driving everybody crazy. They wanted to know where I got my chickens; they didn't look like any that anyone had ever seen. Finally, the secret got out. The others decided they couldn't compete with my chickens, and for a while they stopped having the egg laying contest.

The Small Animals

For the first twenty years of my practice, I took care of large animals—cows, horses, goats, and sheep. Dogs and cats were kind of a sideline. But increasingly, people were acquiring small pets and were willing to pay for veterinary services. I didn't feel confident enough about dog and cat diseases, which meant that I needed to go back to school. I bought all the texts that were available on small animal diseases and started to attend seminars and professional meetings. Then I discovered what a lot of people found out later: I could make three times as much money in one-third the time by having these animals brought in to me. Since I had a big farm and a big house, it occurred to me that I could be holding office hours in the evening for small animals. So, I started a little clinic at the end of my house. My hours at that time were six to eight o'clock at night. I still could get out early in the morning when the farmers started milking their cows at five o'clock, shag around all day, and get home in time for office hours.

Chocolate

Narragansett Pier is a wealthy place. Back then, there was a rail line, and people shipped their polo ponies from New York. We had polo fields here, and we had a very active community of people with homes on Ocean Road overlooking Narragansett Bay. Some of these people were summer residents, some were permanent, and many had small pets.

One of the summer people was Mrs. Barnes Newbury, who lived in a huge house with her staff, her children, and at least six little Dachshunds. When Mrs. Newbury went to bed, the six dogs would go upstairs and jump onto her big canopy bed and get under the covers. Mrs. Newbury often called me to say that one of the dogs was sick. I remember one little brown Dachshund named Chocolate, her favorite. All her dogs were so fat that they could hardly walk; she overfed them constantly, sitting in bed and feeding them off a tray. Whenever they had any problems, nine times out of ten it was from overeating. She would call me and say, "Chocolate did not eat today. I think there is something wrong."

"Mrs. Newbury, I don't know what's wrong. There are several possibilities. Would you let me take Chocolate home with me? My wife and I will find out what is wrong with her."

At home, we would put her in a nice big cage with some fresh water in a bowl, and that is all Chocolate had for three days.

By the third day, Chocolate was ravenous. I would pick her up, put her in my car, and take her to the big house on Ocean Road. The minute the butler opened the door, Chocolate would bound out of my arms, up the stairs, and into the bedroom to the food dish. Mrs. Newbury would be beside herself with joy. She said, "Oh, Doctor, you've done it again." I did that so many times, I figured she'd get wise to me, but she never did. She was a wonderful client, a grand person, and we got along very well.

Pepe and Fifi

Another client, a wealthy dowager named Mrs. Simmons, lived in one of the big houses down at the Pier. She came into the office one evening with her two miniature poodles, one male and one female, Pepe and Fifi. The complaint was that Fifi was becoming very fat and appeared to be bloated. I examined Fifi, and when I palpated her belly, I could feel little lumps that felt very much like puppies.

"Mrs. Simmons, did Fifi have a season recently?"

"Oh, yes, she was in heat."

"How long ago?"

"Oh, five or six weeks ago. Something like that."

"Mrs. Simmons, I think Fifi's pregnant."

"Fifi is not pregnant. She is never, ever out of my sight, and she is always on a leash and so that would be impossible."

"Well, how about Pepe?"

With great indignation, Mrs. Simmons said, "Dr. Kaplan, Pepe and Fifi are brother and sister. He would never do that." I could swear at that moment Pepe's eyes twinkled and his mustache bristled. Needless to say, Fifi had four cute little puppies two weeks later.

The Aggressive Boxer Dog

Broad Rock Farm adjoined my farm; the Gamminos lived there. The youngest son, Michael, had a beautiful Boxer dog. It loved people and was a great dog, but it had a thing for attacking other dogs. I kept telling Michael to have him neutered to get rid of his aggression, but Michael didn't want to do that.

Over time, people brought me a succession of dogs with torn necks and ears, bruises, and all kinds of trauma that had been inflicted by this Boxer. Michael wasn't aware of the number of times people had to bring their dogs to me to be patched up. In one of those fights, apparently the Boxer got his ears torn, and Mike brought the dog in for my attention. When I got done, I said, "You know, Mike, I ought to do this for nothing, because this dog has created an awful lot of business for me, the way he has done a job on so many other dogs."

"Well," Mike said, "I've tried everything. I can't watch him all the time. He gets out of my sight and I do not want to keep him on a chain."

So I suggested, "What he needs is for a dog to give him a good licking, and I mean, really beat up on him, and maybe he won't be so anxious to fight."

"That might be a good idea, but I don't know where you will find a dog like that."

"I have a German Shepherd dog here who outweighs your

dog. Chester is the nicest dog in the world. I've had him since he was a puppy. He loves people. He loves little dogs and big dogs, but he would clean up your Boxer so fast in a fight that it would be over by the count of ten."

"Do you really think it would help?"

"Yes, I do."

"Well, I'd consider that. When do you want to arrange it?"

"Why don't you call me tonight after work, and while it's still light we'll take them out back. I'll make sure neither one gets badly hurt. We'll see if we can teach him a lesson."

Taking advantage of the conditioned reflexes of animals is a great method of training. If a dog gets beaten in a fight, he won't feel dominant. When Mike came over later, with his dog on a choke chain, I brought out Chester, holding his collar. As we walked over toward the Boxer, his whole attitude changed. He started to salivate and growl and the hair on his neck came up. I had seen Chester in action before with aggressive dogs, but I knew there wasn't a dog I ever saw that had a chance against him. Besides, Chester had heavy fur, while the Boxer had very thin fur, hardly any coat at all.

Chester

I said, "We'll get them within ten feet of each other, so they know they're going to fight. When I say, 'One, two three, go,' we'll both let go, and the fight will be over before you know it. I'll make sure that your dog doesn't get hurt too bad."

"Well, I don't believe that."

I counted. The dogs met in midair, went straight up, then hit the ground. Chester rolled the Boxer three or four times, wrapped his legs around him, got him by the throat, and pressed down. The Boxer was screaming, kicking his legs; he was all done.

Mike was hollering, "He's gonna kill him."

I ran over and grabbed Chester and pulled him off. That Boxer lay on the ground for a few minutes. Chester just sat there watching him. Eventually, Mike revived him and got him on his feet. He was kind of wobbly, but when he looked over at Chester, he started to snarl again. I loosened Chester's chain without letting him go. I asked the Boxer, "Do you want to bite again?" He turned away. He didn't have much of a tail, so I can't say he put his tail between his legs, but he went right behind his master, as if to say, "Let's go home." I never saw any more of the Boxer's victims after that.

Bobby's Calf

Ben Brow had a beautiful flat farm in Slocum. He had some of the best Brown Swiss cattle in the country. Ben's son Bobby, with the help of his father, would pick out a calf with great promise as his project to show at the fairs. One time, he had raised an exceptionally nice heifer. Bobby worked her every day: he groomed her, trained, led her, and walked her to get her into championship shape.

One day, while Bobby was at school, the herdsman called me to say that there was an emergency with Bobby's calf. It was convulsing and he was afraid it was dying. He had no idea what happened or what was wrong. She had been fine that morning when Bobby left for school. I rushed right over there. It took me about fifteen minutes driving fast. I ran into the barn, but the calf was dead. The herdsman said, "We'd better find out what happened because if it's something that's contagious or something that might spread to the other calves, we really ought to know. I want you to do everything you can to find out why this calf died."

I proceeded to do a postmortem. I had to remove all the organs, including the liver, heart, and kidneys, and tissues from the intestines and stomachs. I laid all these out very neatly on some feedbags in the stall. I was still not certain of the cause of death, but I thought it might have been an embolism, or blood clot, that had somehow gotten into the general circulation and ended up in the heart. I had just cut the heart open and was examining the heart chambers when Bobby came into the barn. He saw everybody standing around, and he went down to the stall. There was his beautiful calf, in pieces, and Bobby looked at me, looked at the calf, looked at the herdsman, and with tears in his eyes asked, "Is she dead, Doc?" It turned out that the calf had died of a twisted intestine. Poor Bobby. Hard lesson. Hard life lesson.

Hooked!

Labor Day weekend. I had mowed five acres of pasture. It had been a very dry summer. There were a lot of weeds, so it had taken me about three hours. I was having lunch when the phone rang and a woman in a panic told me that her dog had just become tangled in a fishing line, with a large hook in its mouth and another in its paw. She could not reach her regular veterinarian, and wondered if I would help her out. As always has been my policy, I said, "Sure. Bring the dog up."

These hooks were huge steel hooks that were impossible to cut with ordinary cutting pliers, which normally could be used with fresh-water or light hooks. You can't pull back on a hook or you'll tear the flesh. I told the woman that I would have to anesthetize her dog. We then were able to use a metal hacksaw to cut off the ends of the hooks, and force the sharp ends through the skin and remove them. It was a great deal of work but we finally got the job done. The family was very grateful.

Animal Fads

It was amazing to me how many of my clients were into get-rich-quick schemes involving animals. Some sold their farms in order to get into something. A demand would be created by the originators, very similar to a Ponzi scheme. I saw people investing in ostriches, pigmy goats, Arab horses, chinchillas, potbelly pigs, and miniature horses. Despite my attempts at guidance, they went ahead, doomed to failure right from the start. I don't hear much now about making money from animal fads, but I have lots of memories of friends who got caught up in them.

The word was out: ostrich was the meat of the future. It was lean and it was delicious. Ostriches would lay so many eggs and hatch so many young. A couple of my clients started here in Rhode Island and then went to Florida and continued into quite large operations. One of the people I tried to dissuade called me from Florida to tell me his tale of woe. He had one hundred ostriches, and many of them were sitting on fertile eggs when an airplane flew overhead. The ostriches became so frightened from the noise that they pecked at all the eggs and broke them. That was the end of that venture.

Another scheme was for a celebrity to hold a horse auction, where the promoters would get together and bid on each other's horses to get the price way up. Innocent bystanders would be impressed and get taken in.

Potbelly pigs was another fad, and all of a sudden, my clients wanted to get in on it. They were in short supply and commanded high prices, but then within a year or two, you couldn't give them away. Even the animal rescue leagues had potbelly pigs for adoption.

The Chinchilla Scheme

About forty-five years ago, chinchilla raising was supposedly a lucrative business. Chinchillas came from the Andes Mountains in South America and were hard to come by. Some promoters in the United States had cornered the market on importing chinchillas, and they started a big advertising campaign: raise chinchillas in your home and make a lot of money. Chinchillas were as prolific as rabbits, and at that time, costly—$1,500 a pair.

The advertising created such a demand that everybody was trying to get into this new cottage industry; there was a long waiting list. One of the pioneers around here was an elderly woman named Westcote who had a beautiful home on a pond in East Matunuck, near Block Island Sound. She had quietly started accumulating so many chinchillas that she converted half her house to raising them. She couldn't supply the demand, but would occasionally sell a few.

Mrs. Westcote called to ask me if I knew anything about chinchillas. I told her I did not but would be willing to learn. She offered her library and told me that she'd pay my way to a chinchilla meeting. She wanted me to take a real interest and become proficient in chinchilla diseases, which I did.

This was a great, new field, and money was no object. But, when I started to take care of the chinchillas, I found out something quite surprising. Mrs. Westcote told me that a prime chinchilla coat in the New York fur market was worth just $5,000. Then she added that it was very difficult to get a prime chinchilla because they fight and pull their hair out, and that female chinchillas have a habit of killing their young ones. All in all, it sounded to me like a pretty bad business, but the promoters had done a good job, so the demand was unbelievable.

Among those who wanted to get into the chinchilla business was a young Oklahoman named Jasper Albright. Jasper was the head farmer for Jim Beattie, and any time I went to the farm, Jasper would get me aside talking about chinchillas. He was absolutely obsessed with getting chinchillas. The more I tried to discourage him, the more he would tell me that he knew better, if he could just get a pair to get started. He'd heard about my taking care of Mrs. Westcote. I told him, "She doesn't sell that many," and he said "Well, keep me in mind."

At about that time, Mrs. Westcote told me she needed to go into the hospital for some surgery. Not daring to entrust her chinchillas to anybody but me, she asked if she could move all of them to my house. She would send carpenters to build cages and make a proper place for them. Mrs. Westcote said she was not only willing to pay for everything, but she was also willing to give me two pairs of chinchillas with their young if I would agree to do this for as long as it took. I talked it over with my wife, and she said it was okay if I wanted to do it.

The carpenters came and converted the whole basement for the chinchillas, and in due time all the chinchillas moved in. I soon discovered that chinchillas are nocturnal. The little rascals were going to keep us up all night playing and chirping, but we decided that we would get used to it.

Three or four days later, I received a telephone call from Mrs. Westcote, who had good news. She didn't need to go to the hospital after all and wanted her chinchillas back. "Now, my agreement with you was that I would give you two pairs of chinchillas with cages and feeders, so I am going to give them to you in return for your being so kind as to agree to take care of my chinchillas." Now I was stuck with two pairs of chinchillas that I had no interest in, and I was convinced that the chinchilla business was a racket.

"Well, what are you going to do with our new chinchillas?" my wife asked.

I decided to see if Jasper Albright was still interested in buying them. "Jasper, I've got an answer to your dreams." I said I would be willing to sell the chinchillas and all that went with them for $1,000. Jasper was beside himself—he was not only getting a bargain but he would be able to get started in the business. When I told my wife, she said, "I don't know why you don't just give the chinchillas to Jasper."

"Well, I figure on giving him a real break."

"But it isn't right, if he gets stuck with them."

When Jasper told us that he had to borrow the money to pay for the chinchillas, my wife got really upset. "Now, he's going to have to pay the bank, and he's stuck with these useless animals that you, yourself, have said were not going to be worth five dollars each when the bottom falls out."

I listened to that for two or three days, and then I said, "Look, you put the money away in a safe place, and if Jasper gets stuck, I'll give him his money back."

A few days went by and I thought I'd stop in and see Jasper. He was out, but his wife was there. She showed me where the cages were, but there was only one pair of chinchillas. "What happened to the other pair?" I asked her.

"Oh, Jasper sold them."

"What did he get for them?"

"$1,500."

So much for feeling sorry for Jasper. I went home and told my wife, "You know, there are no flies on that old Okie."

Years later, whenever I saw Jasper, I'd tell him, "That's one of my favorite stories." Jasper just chuckled. "Well, I figured if I did that," he said, "I'd have a profit, and then, I could have the other pair and breed them." Sure enough, it wasn't a year before the market collapsed, and you couldn't give those little animals away.

A Matter of Beliefs

One time, a man came to my office with a nice English Setter and told me that he wanted to have the dog put to sleep, that he was going south and didn't want to take the dog along. The man was a summer resident and had never been to me before.

I said, "But he's a nice dog. Why would you want to put him to sleep?"

"Well, he's got this skin condition and he has no hair and he's scratching all the time, so I think it's best that we put him to sleep."

"No, I don't think so. He's a nice dog, and if you took him over to the Animal Rescue League, they would find a home for him and take care of his skin condition. It wouldn't be that big a problem."

"No. I've decided I'm going to put the dog to sleep."

"Well, it's not my policy to put healthy dogs to sleep, and I'm just not going to be able to do it."

"Well, I don't understand. He's my dog. I'm willing to pay you to do it, and if you'll just do it, I'll take care of burying him, or you can bury him for me up here, if you want, or whatever."

"No, I'm not going to do it. It's just not my policy. I'm very reluctant to euthanize even old dogs; I have to be convinced that they're suffering and that it's for their own good."

Again the owner repeated, "He's my dog and I think I have the right to put him to sleep."

"Well, you do have that right, but you're going to have to take him somewhere else, because I won't do it."

There were people waiting in the office and I needed to get

rid of this man. I stood there for a moment, and then I had what I thought was a pretty good idea. I looked him in the eye and said, "I'll tell you the real reason that I won't do it. It's against my religion, and you certainly wouldn't want me to go against my religion, would you?"

"Okay."

On his way out, he turned around and asked me, "Would you mind telling me what your religion is?"

I was at the end of my rope, but I contained myself and said, "It's none of your business. Now, get out of here."

With that, he grabbed the dog and went to his car. I went in the house to share this tale with my wife; we couldn't get over it, that my excuse to the dog owner was enough to send him packing. I never did find out what happened to that poor dog, but it was a good way to get rid of a difficult client, and I still think of this encounter when I'm having to discuss euthanasia and whether it would be best for the animal.

Admiral George

At one time, I had my own stallion, and I went from having one mare to having three mares that I selected as the basis of my breeding program. I am fortunate to have raised some very nice horses and to have won quite a few races with them. We had two tracks here on the farm: a little turf course, and a quarter-mile oval in one of the big fields. We would give the horses their early training on the small ring. First, we would drive them, and then, they were "mouthed," to respond to pressure on the reins. In other words, we gave them their first training on the ground, and then worked up to walking and trotting, and finally canter-ing and galloping. It was a long process.

The most fun was with the young horses, and we could tell early on whether a horse was going to be a good one. One par-ticular horse, Admiral George, showed promise from the start. As he progressed, we were more and more convinced that this was an outstanding horse. He turned out to be the New England champion. He was so good that I had to ship him out of New England to Maryland and some of the bigger tracks because there was no competition for him here.

I had quite a few friends who were interested in horses. One, Martin Anderson, lived in Hope Valley. He was an avid follower of racehorses, and whenever he had a chance, he would wait up at Jack Morgan's diner, which was frequented by all the locals in Hope Valley. Martin was always after me to let him know when I had a horse that was going to win, because he wanted to bet on him, but I wouldn't give out information about my horses. However, Martin knew that Jack and I were friends, so he was always pumping Jack for information.

We finally got Admiral George ready to run. His first start

was going to be at Rockingham Park, and we were confident that he would win the first time out. Martin went to work in the morning and then pretended he was sick, so he could get up to the racetrack. When I went into the paddock, there were quite a few people out in front of the stalls. Martin Anderson was right there in the front row. I looked over and thought, "Well, he got the word and he's here to bet on Admiral George."

In the next stall was a beautiful big black horse. There must have been ten people in the stall with him, including a priest. Everybody was excited. The horse had flowers in his mane and tail and was prancing around. He looked just beautiful. Everybody in the paddock crowd was attracted to this gorgeous horse, and then, they paraded him before the race. He was impressive. My trainer and I looked over at the beautiful horse with the entourage, and said, "That horse looks like a runner, and he'd better be or he's not going to beat Admiral George."

In the race, Admiral George went all out; he just galloped and galloped. He won and we all had our picture taken. When I came out of the winner's circle, Martin was standing there with a very woeful look on his face. He said, "Oh, Doctor, I made such an effort to come up here. I came up here to bet on your horse, but that horse in the next stall was so beautiful, I couldn't take my eyes off it and all those people, so I bet on that horse."

"Oh, that's too bad, Martin."

"Well, you don't know how bad I feel."

So, of course, I couldn't resist that old joke: "Martin, you know why that priest was there? To give that horse the last rites!"

That same day, Burton Froburg, the former URI basketball star and farmer, was also at the race. He didn't know anything about racing, except that he was interested in my horses. He had never been to a race or even been on a horse. I had told him I was going up to Rockingham Park to see my horse, Admiral George, run. So, curious, he and his wife, Rhoda, took the day off and drove up to Rockingham Park to their first race, and, of course, Admiral George won and paid a big price.

Burt and Rhoda were in the winner's circle with our friends, all of whom had bet on the horse. Burt, who had been in a lot of exciting athletic events, said, "This is one of the best days I've ever had." That told me he had bet a little, but I didn't know how much until later on, when I was at his farm, and he invited me into the house and showed me his brand new refrigerator and stove. "How do you like those? Compliments of Admiral George."

Burt's mother, who was from the old country, Sweden, had prepared a special treat for me, and she brought out a bowl of the most delicious, special egg and milk pudding and kept offering me more and more. I ate almost the whole bowl. When I finished, I told her, "Mrs. Froburg, that's the best pudding I've ever eaten in my life. What's it made out of?"

"Oh, that's made out of fresh cow's milk."

When a cow freshens, or has a calf, for the first few days she produces a very thick substance called colostrum, which is full of all kinds of antibodies that give the new calf immunity. Normally, I wouldn't have eaten it. I had no idea. After she told me, I left and went around behind the barn and threw up.

The Records Brothers and the Circus

The Records brothers were part of a large family of farmers. Larry Records was a state senator and a national officer in the Ayrshire Breeders Association, a wonderful person with a beautiful family. Sometimes I had breakfast with the family when I was there early in the morning, and I considered them good friends.

Larry had two nephews who were crazy about circuses. They went as far as New York to the Barnum & Bailey Circus and followed it to Providence and Boston. We had some little fairs around here, and those boys built miniature circuses out of wood and made miniature animals and circus wagons and rings, which they exhibited at the fairs. They were works of art. They had their own little tent, and they always said they were going to have their own circus when they got older.

When they grew up, they decided they would have a circus with live animals, like a petting zoo. At their little farm in Hope Valley, they talked to me quite a bit and asked if I would take care of their animals. I told them that although I really didn't know anything about elephants and camels, I'd be willing to get some textbooks, go to a meeting or two, and maybe visit the zoo in Boston to talk to the zookeeper.

Sure enough, they acquired an Asian elephant, which they named Sam. He was a young elephant from Benson's Wild Animal Farm in New Hampshire. They had worked with the elephant keeper there and learned various ways to train elephants. When they heard that Benson's had an extra elephant for sale, the boys got the money together for the start of their own zoo. They were on their way to having their circus. They built a special pen for their elephant and then went around to the fairs and gave elephant rides in parking lots. They trained Sam to stand on one leg, stand on a barrel, and balance a ball on the end of his trunk.

One bitter, stormy morning, they called me. There had been a big snowstorm with high winds. The window in Sam's pen had blown open, and all the cold air and snow had come in on their elephant. He was sneezing, he had mucus running out of his eyes, and he was coughing. Obviously, he had pneumonia. At this point, I had never treated zoo animals, but I had read about elephants and treating them. I was a bit concerned about giving Sam an injection. I learned that, as far as injections went, there was a soft place in the armored hide on the hind leg. Penicillin was the principal antibiotic that we used then for respiratory problems or pneumonia.

But I didn't know how Sam would react. I asked, "What does Sam do when he's hurt or mad or defending himself?"

"He swings his trunk like a hose. He can cut you in half with that trunk."

"We're going to have to figure out some way to do this, so Sam won't turn on me and cut me in half."

I had an idea: "If you get Sam to stand on the barrel with his front leg, he'll put the hind leg straight out with his trunk up in the air. I'll get behind him and give him the needle before he knows what happened." If you can picture it, that's exactly what happened. I found that little soft spot and sank in that needle as quick as I could. Sam never moved a muscle. So, I got out of there with my life, and Sam responded to the treatment and got over the cold. He was fine.

Next, the boys were determined to get a hippopotamus. They had heard of some extra hippos at a zoo in Ohio. They called me, all excited, and told me they had a hippo coming in and wanted me to be on call in case anything happened to the hippo in transit. The hippo was shipped in a wooden crate on a special truck. Somehow during the trip, the hippo's back had become scraped and infected, and there was quite a nasty wound where he had been bumping up against the boards on the top of the crate. His whole back was bleeding, and I didn't have any knives big enough or strong enough to deal with the wounded flesh, but we had to figure out a way to get at him. They took a couple of the boards off the top of the crate and there still wasn't room enough, so they took off all the boards, which left the top open. We were all leaning over the crate and trying to deal with the dead flesh and get it to a point where we could treat it with some antibiotics and wound stimulus to try to get it to heal—at least that was my plan. But while we were leaning on the crate, the hippo started rocking back and forth; the crate turned over on its side and out came the hippo.

The three of us started running around the barn with the hippo chasing us. One of the boys got a big, heavy rope. The hippo was infuriated, he was scared, and he had those big jaws. He could have broken us in half if he got us. We had no place to go. Finally, one of the boys got the rope around his neck and wrapped it around a pole in the barn. The hippo ran around and around the pole and pulled it down. Half the floor above came down on top of us. We finally got enough ropes on him. We were all exhausted, including the hippo, but we managed to get him into the pen the boys had prepared for him. But how were we going to be able to handle this hippo? We couldn't get near him to do anything.

We needed help, so I decided to call the zookeeper at the Franklin Park Zoo in Boston. "Oh, yeah," he said, "that's a common problem with hippos. If you want me to come down, I will. We can shoot a dart into him and put him under anesthesia so we can work on him." So, he came down and tranquilized the hippo. Then, we spent about an hour trimming and cleaning the wound. The hippo recovered and he was with the brothers for a long time.

The Camel's Abscess

During World War II, Dr. Ian "Mac" McClelland served for the British. He was stationed in Egypt, where he had the experience of taking care of King Farouk's camels. Afterwards, he established a veterinary practice here in East Greenwich. Rocky Point Park was nearby in Warwick, and there was a carnival featuring zoo animals. It came as no surprise that, when the camel imported for the occasion had an infection that needed treatment, Mac would get the call. By then, Mac had retired, so he turned to me. He assured me that I would be able to handle the job with no trouble; all I needed to do was read up on the care of camels.

Camels are pretty nasty when they are stirred up or threatened, and this camel had developed a huge abscess under his throat. One of the ways camels protect themselves is to spit, and they spit projectiles like rubber bullets.

I said to the staff at the park, "I don't know how we're going to do this. Can you get a rope on him and take him outside? Then we'll see if we can get to that big tree out there and run the rope around the tree trunk a few times with a slip knot on the camel's neck, and snug him up against the tree."

We enticed him with a little food, and got the rope over his neck and around the tree. With that, the camel pulled back against the rope, which choked him enough so I could come in close. I didn't realize until then how big that abscess was. So I decided I might as well make a big incision; I came down about eight to ten inches, and the pus exploded, covering me from head to foot. You can imagine how I smelled. They offered to let me take a shower and lend me some clothes, but I declined and went home.

Fortunately for me, my wife had no sense of smell. When we first started going out together, she told me that she had lost her sense of smell. I figured that was an asset. "You'd make a good veterinarian's wife, if you can't smell," I told her. The camel's abscess was a good example. So, I put on fresh clothes every day. She made sure that I always had plenty of fresh clothes. She wasn't taking any chances.

My Honor System

I don't send bills. Everything is on the honor system, and it's always been that way. A very well dressed man walked in one day and said that he represented a bill collection service. He wanted to enroll me as a customer and said he had a high collection rate. I said, "No, and before you go any further, so we don't waste your time or my time either, I've been in practice for almost fifty years, and I'm not owed five cents, so I really don't need your services."

He looked at me as if he'd never heard of such a thing, so I said, "That's strange to you, isn't it?"

"Yes, it is, frankly."

"Well, my policy has always been the honor system. If you don't have any money, why, that's okay. Just as long as you're up front about it, and you've got a sick animal, we'll take care of it for you. And when we get done, we'll tell you how much it is, and when you're able, you come by and pay."

I would treat the animal, and the client would tell me, "Send me a bill," and I would say, "I don't send bills. You know what you owe me, and I'm going to put your name down." I had a big copybook. I would write down the name, the date, and the amount. That honor system worked pretty well, especially in the beginning, when there were so many military families who had small pets and had to watch their pennies. That was my system over sixty years of practice.

Over the years, I have had many people come in and pay me money that I don't have any record of. In fact, I once got a check for a hundred dollars, with a little note of apology enclosed. I had completely forgotten why the person owed me, because I hadn't put it in the book and I hadn't sent a bill, but that was my honor system.

An Honest Man

I was mowing my lawn one Sunday morning a long time ago when a pickup truck came barreling into my driveway. The driver, obviously distraught, jumped out of his car, ran over to me, and asked me if I was the doctor.

"My dog was just hit by a car. I put him in the truck. I couldn't get anybody because it's Sunday. Could you please take care of him?"

"Sure." I got my stethoscope and listened to the dog. He appeared to be in shock with possible internal bleeding, but a lot of the other signs were good and I thought that I could help him. I got my bag, came back to the pickup, and treated the dog. We waited a while and then I checked his pulse, heart, and respiration. I told the man, "I've done all I can for him, but I'd like you to hang around here for a half hour or so, in case I need to treat him further. I'll be cutting the lawn right here. You just keep an eye on him."

Every once in a while, I would come back, and the dog seemed to have come to. He was holding his head up. His breathing was better. His color had returned. His mucous membranes looked good. The man stayed for probably an hour. The dog had really come to and struggled to his feet. I said, "He's going to be all right."

The dog's owner was a man of color. He told me his name, and he said, "You know some of my family, my brother. I live in Wood River Junction."

"Sure, I recognize the name."

"I rushed out of the house when this happened, and I didn't bring any money with me. I'll get paid next Friday. I'll come back on Friday and pay you. How much is it?"

I told him, and he said, "Now, I'm really grateful. I'll be back. You can trust me."

"I know I can trust you. I'll tell you what. If you don't come back, you'll have the distinction of being the only man of color who didn't keep his word and didn't pay his bill."

He looked at me with kind of a bemused expression and said, "Well, I'll see you." He got in his truck and he left. The dog was all right.

The following Friday, in he came to the office and waited his turn. "I owe you for taking care of my dog and I'm here to pay you." Then he looked at me and asked, "Well, the record is still clear; isn't it?"

"It sure is."

"I've been thinking about this all week. Did you tell me this just to make sure I'd come back or is that the truth?"

"No, I never thought to ensure your coming back by telling you a story like that. It just happens to be true."

"Well, I'm grateful, and I'll be back for other stuff and so will other members of my family."

Professional Courtesy

In 1958 or thereabouts, the Sturges estate (formerly the home of T. P. Hazard's sister) was purchased by the Catholic Diocese of Providence to establish a school for girls, Mount St. Joseph's College. The grounds contained a beautiful Georgian style home, which became the residence for the teaching nuns. In the meantime, I had built my own stable and was no longer using the Sturges's stable. When the nuns arrived, they brought along a flock of sheep, and, of course, as I was living right across the road, I was asked if I would inspect the sheep and be their veterinarian. From that point on, I had a very nice relationship with the nuns.

I had a policy that I would never charge a member of the clergy, priest, minister, rabbi, or sachem. I felt an obligation to treat their animals and not charge them. A high moral code was instilled in me by my parents and reinforced at the University of Pennsylvania, where ethics was a very strong subject, so I did not charge professional people, which included doctors and dentists (but not lawyers).

Dr. White, the only dentist in Wakefield at the time, on Main Street, had a small farm. His specialty was show chickens, which he took around to various exhibits. He also raised dogs and I was his veterinarian. I never charged Doc White, and my family never paid a dental bill. The same went for the physician in town. There were two physicians, and the one I became very friendly with was Dr. Jack Turco, who was not only a very good person but an excellent doctor. I took care of his animals and never paid a doctor bill.

So of course I took care of the sheep for the nuns and the

first time I visited I told them there was no charge. Within a week or so, Sister Superior, an elderly Irish nun with a great sense of humor (like many of the Irish, I've found) called me and said, "Doctor, we have an old sheep here who is on his last legs, and I wonder if you would slaughter this sheep for us and maybe help us to skin the sheep and butcher him, so that we can have meat on the table."

"Sister, I don't see anything wrong with him except old age. He's going to be pretty tough to eat."

"Well," the sister said, "we don't see very much meat around here, and believe me, when the sisters are eating that sheep, they'll think they died and went to heaven." So I slaughtered the sheep for her, and I'm sure that the good sisters disposed of it in short order.

Near the stable, they had gardens where they raised their own vegetables and flowers and other plants. But the well that supplied the animals had gone dry. The nuns were hauling water from the big house, which was not only cumbersome but quite a distance and not enough to satisfy a flock of thirsty sheep. I asked Sister Superior what they were going to do for water.

"Well, the younger nuns had been dropping miraculous medals down the well in the hope that it would rejuvenate."

"Do you think that's going to help, Sister?"

"I think we're going to have to call the well driller."

That was right to the point.

As I got to know the people at Mount St. Joseph's, I was asked by one of the nuns if I'd be interested in teaching a hygiene course. I love teaching but I'd never really had an opportunity to teach in a formal setting. She told me that there were certain requirements for a teaching certificate, about nine credits in education courses, just a formality.

I discovered that they were easy courses and that I would have to go back to school—not a problem, because the courses were only three hours a week and taught at the University of Rhode Island, only a few minutes away. I enrolled in my first course, Materials and Methods of Classroom Learning. I was assured it was an easy course. When I reported to the class, I found myself among a bunch of 18-year-old freshmen. The professor felt that this course wouldn't be any trouble for me, even though I had been out of college for twenty-some years. As the class went on, I found that the professor would defer to me. Everyone was very respectful.

The textbooks were late, and for three or four weeks we had only the notes that we took in class. The professor told us that he would have to give his first exam based on our class notes and the first three chapters in the textbook. I read the chapters and outlined them. Because of the amount of material, the professor gave a true–false exam. It was a two-hour exam, and I breezed through it in about forty-five minutes. I got up, the first one by far to finish, and laid my paper on the desk.

"How was it?" he asked

"Well, for me, it was pretty easy."

The others were only halfway through the exam; they probably figured, that, considering my education and my age, it was no wonder that I found the exam to be easy.

A couple of weeks later, after the professor had corrected the exams, he explained that, as he returned the papers, he would call our names and give a number, which he would explain after he had given out all the papers. He started out alphabetically, the first person got a ten, the next one got a twelve, the next one got a fifteen, and somebody got a seven or eight. He went through the whole list; my name came up with thirty-two. Well, that was far and away the highest score and I was pretty pleased. He got down to the last person, and then he said, "Now, the number that you recorded is the number of questions you got wrong."

I went up to see him after the class and I told him that there was no way, that I knew that course cold, I understood everything.

"It must be that your true–false questions were ambiguous."

"Let's go over some of the questions."

At the next class, he announced that he felt it wasn't a fair examination and offered a way for the students to adjust their scores, which was all right with me. I got through that course, and, as I remember, I didn't get an A, but I got a passing grade. After that, I took two more courses, which made me eligible for my teaching certificate.

Once I had the certificate, the nuns wanted to discuss how much they were going to pay me, which was a problem because they were on a limited budget. I told them that I would teach the course for my own gratification. The school was right across the road from me and the teaching didn't involve that many hours a week. I just enjoyed working with the young people.

The Power of Prayer

When word got around that I didn't charge members of the clergy, all their cats and dogs were brought to me. The monsignor at Mount St. Joseph's College had two Siamese cats that he thought the world of. When the cats had kittens, he distributed them to his friends and I took care of them, too.

One really funny incident occurred when two nuns came into my office with a sick cat. One sister said, "Doctor, how much do I owe you?"

"Oh, that's all right, Sister, I don't charge members of the clergy,"

She turned to the other nun and said, "See, Sister? I told you we went to the wrong place."

It happened they had mistakenly gone to a veterinarian up the road and were charged at the going rate. Then she realized what she had said, and before she could say anything, I teased, "So, that's the reason you're here, Sister, because I'm free?"

"Oh, Doctor, I'm so sorry, I didn't mean it the way it came out." They apologized profusely, and she said, "Doctor, I'm going to keep you in my prayers."

Every Christmas after that, I got hand-knit sweaters and shawls and socks. And, for as long as they were there, until the college finally closed, I had the nuns and a monsignor praying for me. "That can only help," I thought.

There was a young minister in town by the name of Larry Washburn. He was a farm boy, and pretty soon after he arrived, he found some nice property and raised animals there, especially horses. One day he asked me to look at a lame horse, and while I was there, he showed me a good looking, big, Quarter horse-type gelding. "I got this horse for the kids," he said, "but they don't ride him. He's just standing around here. He's a nice horse, a good riding horse. I keep telling them I'm going to sell him, and I've made up my mind. Do you know anybody who would be interested?"

"Yes, as a matter of fact, I do. I know a fellow who runs a riding academy in East Greenwich, name of Ray LaVoisier. I'll call Ray and see if we can get this horse sold for you."

"Oh, Doctor, if you can do that for me, I'll pray for you the rest of your life."

I thought that was pretty good.

I called Ray, and he and his wife, Laura, went to Larry's that same day because they were looking for that type of horse. The price was right, and I assured them that the horse was nice, gentle, and sound. Laura rode the horse and loved him. About a month or two went by, and I was at the local coffee shop, Phil's, the only restaurant in town. I was down at the far end of the counter when Larry walked in. I was just finishing, and as I went by him on my way out, I leaned over and put my hand on his shoulder.

"You're praying for me aren't you, Larry?"

He looked at me with a blank expression as if to say, "Why in the world is he asking me if I'm praying for him?"

I kept looking at him, waiting, and all of a sudden it dawned on him.

"Oh, oh, oh, yes, I certainly am. I certainly am."

"Thanks a lot, Larry."

That was a source of a lot of joking between the two of us over the years.

Larry always wanted to sail, and after he retired he got a sailboat. He and his wife didn't sail around the world, but they went down the Intercoastal Waterway to Florida and then to the Caribbean. When they got back, they went home to the farm, where some of the kids still kept horses. Their daughter had a horse she wanted me to look at. When I stopped by, she said, "Dad's home. He'll want to see you."

"Hello, Doctor, how do you feel?"

"I feel great, Larry. I feel wonderful."

"See?" he quipped.

Lloyd Whitford was active in the Perryville Baptist Church. All the farmers were church-going, God-fearing people. The church was the center of everything, and Lloyd was one of the pioneers in building a new Bible church for Perryville. Earlier, Lloyd had hired young divinity graduates from the Bible College in Providence. They served as apprentices in Perryville and Lloyd employed them on his farm. So I got to meet these eager young men, and we would engage in conversations about the Bible. If you weren't the same religion as they were, they would try to show you the benefits of their religion.

Reverend Sutton was one of my favorite eager beavers. He would look for me at the farm so that he could ask me if I'd been reading the Bible, as the main occupation in those times was to read the Bible at night—there was no TV then, just radio. According to him, if you wanted to know anything, the answer was in the Bible, and he could quote anything from memory at the drop of a hat. He was really wound up that day.

At that time, the Southern Baptists and the Northern Baptists were split right down the middle. They were having a big battle over segregation; the Southern Baptists didn't want people of color in their churches. They would have their own churches. The Northern Baptists were more liberal in that respect. Reverend Sutton started in, in his usual way, and I commented, "The Southern Baptists and the Northern Baptists are fighting. This has become a major problem in the church and I want to ask you something. I want you to quote me and tell me where in the Bible it says that people of color are not allowed in your churches."

"Well," Sutton looked at me, "well."

This threw him, and he walked away and then turned around with a perplexed look on his face.

"I'm waiting Reverend."

In the meantime, I was working on the cows, and he was pondering. He came back fully five minutes later, and he didn't have an answer. Looking right into my eyes, he said, "Listen, I'm thinking about it. You know, they say the devil was clever."

"So, in other words, you're calling me a devil."

"Well, you proposed a devilish question for me."

We joked about that for years. I think the Baptists have since settled that matter.

Years ago, a young rabbi, Mark Jagolinzer, who had just graduated from Brown University, got his first assignment in Newport. His parents were my clients. Mark was an animal lover and had a couple of dogs. He started bringing the dogs across the Bay to me, which was quite a ride, but he brought his dogs to me for their entire lives, and, of course, I never charged him. His dogs are now buried in my little pet cemetery that I have here for my friends and my own dogs. The dogs that are here have little monuments that were made by a Westerly man who cuts the stone, using mostly Westerly granite, which is quite famous for its quality. I'm still taking care of that graveyard. I like to joke that I've covered all my bases. I can't miss going to heaven.

Horse Auctions

Horse auctions are held in various parts of the country, but the most famous are at Lexington, Kentucky, at Keeneland; the other premier sale of top-quality racehorses is at Saratoga, New York. During the 1960s, I had a trainer, an ex-rider named Richard DeStasio, later one of the top trainers in New York. He had a client who owned a chain of department stores and was interested in purchasing some horses at a certain dispersal sale. DeStasio had heard that there was a famous trainer and owner who was in ill health and selling all his horses at this sale. He asked if I would go to that sale and bid on some horses for his client.

This client and his accountant had decided that he was paying Uncle Sam too much in taxes. He was in a high tax bracket, and at that time, you could deduct all the expenses of owning and racing horses. Like most wealthy people I've ever met, he was interested in saving on taxes. He was a horse lover and he was willing to pay me a commission to go to Saratoga to buy some horses. He called Humphrey Finney, the head of the sales company, and authorized me to bid on his behalf. Now, in that sale, there was an outstanding horse that had won most of his races as a two-year-old and was being mentioned as one of the early favorites for the Kentucky Derby. He was a gray horse named Exhibitionist. I was authorized to bid $200,000 for Exhibitionist, a huge sum of money at that time. All the announcements and write-ups for the sale said that Exhibitionist would top the sale, and $200,000 seemed a likely bid for us to get this horse.

A roommate of mine at the University of Pennsylvania for a time had been Manny Gilman, who became a long-time racetrack veterinarian for the New York Racing Association. He was considered an expert on measurements of famous horses and locomotion, and was probably as well known as any veterinarian in the country at the time. The day before the auction, I went to see Manny and told him I would be bidding on some horses and asked if he could help me weed out any that he wouldn't recommend. This would be a great edge for us. He said Exhibitionist was a nice horse, and he marked out some other horses for me.

I looked up Mr. Finney at the sales company office and introduced myself. "Oh, yes," he said, "we have authorization for you to bid, so anything you bid is okay. I understand you're interested in Exhibitionist? You know, there's a reserve bid on him, $200,000." This meant that the bidding would start at $200,000.

I asked to use his phone and called my client to explain that, by coincidence, the limit we had set was exactly what the reserve was on the horse. "Do you think he's worth $200,000?" he asked me.

"Not of my money, he isn't,"

There was a long silence on the other end and he asked, "What do you mean by that?"

"Well, I'll tell you. Just before I came up here, I went on a call to see a sick cow. I traveled forty miles to get there and back, and with everything included, the charge to that farmer was fifteen dollars. That's real money. The money you're talking about, you told me, is tax money. I wouldn't pay my hard-earned money. I wouldn't pay $10,000 for a horse. Horses are too fragile; you can insure them, but they can go out for a gallop and break a leg. I wouldn't even begin to think of investing that kind of money in a horse.

"So," the client said, "let's forget it."

I was going to get ten percent for going up there, and what I said did me out of a nice commission, but I ended up buying him more than $100,000 worth of horses. Fortunately, they all turned out very well. He was very successful.

Travels Abroad

In the early 1950s, I published an article in the *Journal of Veterinary Medicine* about treating epilepsy in horses with phenobarbital, then in use for people, and not yet recorded anywhere else for use in horses. There are other drugs now, but phenobarbital is still one of the drugs of choice. The article was picked up by a European veterinary journal, and as a result I was invited to appear on a panel in Cambridge, England. This was our first trip outside of the United States.

It was during summer vacation and my wife and I stayed at King George's College in an English dormitory. The furnishings were spartan, to say the least, and men and women were required to be housed separately. Each room was equipped with a narrow bed, and in the middle of the night I heard a tap at the door. Evalyn was there in the hall, unable to get to sleep by herself, so we pulled her bed into my room and all was well. In the morning, I went to the meeting and returned to the room to pick up something. There was the housekeeping department, all atwitter. What fun. We thoroughly enjoyed England and the Newmarket racing scene.

During the 1960s, I was asked by a client if I would be interested in going to Ireland to look at some horses for him. Irish racehorses were just starting to come over to this country and racing very successfully. You could buy a nice racehorse over there for a fraction of what it would cost in the United States, even with the transportation. It seemed like a good opportunity because I'd never been to Ireland. This was the first of quite a few trips to Ireland. My wife and I would always go with the purpose of combining a vacation with looking at horses and possibly purchasing some.

I had a letter of introduction to two prominent Irish veterinarians, the Cosgrove brothers, Maxi and Stan. Maxi ran the Irish National Stud, and Stan was a practicing racetrack veterinarian who had lectured in this country at several of the equine meetings that I had attended.

With the letter of introduction, I went to the Irish National Stud, just outside Dublin, and introduced myself to Dr. Cosgrove. I mentioned some of the people who had referred me to him. That became the beginning of a nice friendship. He showed me the various stallions and horses at the Irish National Stud, and then asked us to the house to meet his wife and have some refreshment.

He had a magnificent house. The bar was elaborate, with all the appropriate furnishings—dartboards and pool tables. It was between mealtimes and he invited me to have a drink. Well, I've never been a drinker. Beer, once in a while, but hard liquor I've never indulged in except for one thing, Irish Mist, which I do enjoy (it had been introduced to me by my friend Jack Morgan). So I did know the taste, the color, and the smell of Irish Mist.

When Dr. Cosgrove asked me what I would have, I asked if he had any Irish Mist. He pulled out a bottle from behind the bar and poured it. My wife had ginger ale. As he poured the Irish Mist, I looked at it. It didn't have any color. It looked like water. I picked it up and smelled it and it had no smell, and I tasted it and it tasted like water, and I said, "Maxi, this doesn't taste like Irish Mist."

"It doesn't? Let me see that. Well, I'll be damned. That's water. That little devil of a daughter of mine, she's gone and poured all my whiskey down the drain and filled the bottles with water." We had a big laugh over that.

Later during that same trip, he gave me an introduction to the most famous trainer of his time, Vincent O'Brien. We made enough contacts to be able to get several leads on some pretty nice horses. Ireland was for me a beautiful country—the people, their warmth, and their friendliness. Horses are a passion with the Irish. They have a completely different type of racing in that they race only one or two days a week, and they race on grass rather than dirt. Most of the wagering is done by handbooks, a completely different kind of wagering from anything I'd ever seen. People set up shop, put up little signs, and give odds on the different horses.

I've had the privilege of going to the races in South America, Argentina and Brazil. I've been to the races in Italy, Germany, England, France, Denmark, and other countries, just about any place where there's horse racing. Of all the racing that I have seen, nothing compared to the atmosphere, excitement, and the whole scene of Irish racing.

Archie Rose and the Races

Archie Rose was a hard-working, intelligent man, a farmer most of his life until he took the job as caretaker at Casey Farm, which suited him just fine. He was free to make any amount of money he wanted to by raising cows, beef, and chickens. In return for free rent, he showed the historic property on certain days and entertained school groups.

Archie was a sportsman. He liked to go to the fights and went to the various sports events at the university, but he didn't know anything about horse racing. He knew that I had horses and took care of horses, so he was always after me to give him a tip on a horse.

"Archie, it's tough betting on horses; I don't know when they are going to win, and where would you bet anyhow?"

He told me that there was a bookmaker at the Elks Club in East Greenwich. "All the Elks play the horses. The bookie comes in and takes the bets, they get the results, and he pays the winners and keeps the money from the losers. I go over there at noon, and they'll take money on any horse. So, if you have a good horse, how about giving me a tip?"

"I don't want to do that, Archie," but he kept after me.

A client of mine, Felix Poncelet, had a horse named Supro, and the trainer had managed to hide a lot of his workouts. This was completely legitimate if you had a horse that was training well, as long as you weren't trying to get a big price on the horse by not allowing him to do his best, which, of course, is strictly illegal. Anyone caught at that kind of thing could be barred from racing. Supro was training exceptionally well, and he was about to make his first start, at Narragansett Park. Since I had been treating him, I certainly was going to go to the track and watch him. Now, I didn't routinely bet on horses, but since I always took an interest in the horses I took care of, I would be willing to take a little chance. I was impressed with Supro.

I came rushing home from my calls, took a shower, and changed my clothes. About then, the phone rang. Archie Rose had a cow with mastitis and wanted me to take care of it. I had plenty of time, so I took off my jacket and put on a pair of coveralls, but otherwise I was dressed well, obviously not in the usual farm clothes. Archie noticed and asked where I was going. I told him a friend of mine was running a horse at Narragansett Park.

"Is he going to win?"

"I don't know, Archie, he's training well, and I really think he'll run fine, but I don't know that he will win."

He asked for the name of the horse, and I told him.

"Well then, I'll go to the Elks Club and bet a little."

There were a lot of good horses in the race and nobody was betting on Supro. The odds were thirty-five to one, which meant that a two-dollar bet would return seventy if he won. The owner and I bet on him, and he led almost all the way. It was his first start, and he got tired at the end; another horse beat him at the wire, which meant that Supro finished second. Because he was such a long shot and the horse that beat him was also a long shot, he paid over thirty dollars on a two-dollar bet to place, and also a lot of money to show. But we had bet on him to win, which didn't do much good for us. We were disappointed, but that's the way racing is.

I went home and got ready for office hours. Three or four people were there with dogs and cats, and pretty soon Archie Rose's car pulled up. He came into my office, obviously in very good humor. He reached into his pocket and took out a big roll of bills, fifties and hundreds. "How do you like that for my first bet? I made a bundle, and you are entitled to any part of it."

"You won all this money on Supro? Tell me exactly how you bet on this horse."

This is how he related it to me. He plopped down $200 and said to the bookie, "Place $200 on Supro. Since "place" means second, and Supro came in second, Archie was a big winner.

I refused to take any of the money. I had to explain to Archie that he was the luckiest man in the world having won all that money that way. He agreed and decided that winning money at the races was a lot better than working. He started getting the racing papers, bought a pair of binoculars, and began going to the races every day. It wasn't much later that Archie lost all the money and then some. I told him, "Archie, there is an old saying in racing: 'You can beat the race, but you can't beat the races.' The odds are against you, and if you keep playing, you are going to lose."

Archie MacLaughlin

Archie MacLaughlin ran the Casey Farm after Archie Rose died. Archie found some baby crows abandoned in a nest and brought them into the barn. The crow has a split tongue, which enables it to speak, and Archie taught this one to speak. The crow went everywhere, perched on Archie's shoulder. Everybody knew the crow and Archie, and people would stop just to hear the crow speak. When the ladies in the historical society came to visit and inspect the farm, they would have tea and cake and the crow would hop around from person to person, begging for food. Often it would get sick from eating too much, and Archie would know what to do.

Then one day, I went over and the crow wasn't around. I asked Archie, "Where is the crow?" Archie told me that the crow was dead. He said that his daughter Lizzie had come home for a visit and saw the crow sitting on a stone wall, his head down. Her father explained that the guests had overfed the crow. She volunteered to take him to the new bird specialist in Wickford, but her father told her to leave the crow alone, he'd be all right. But Lizzie took the crow to the bird specialist.

A couple of hours later, Lizzie came back with the crow, dead. Archie bawled her out and said, "What in the world happened? I told you to leave that crow alone; it's happened to him before."

"I don't know. The man put a tube down its throat to give it some liquid and the crow just keeled over and died."

"He probably put the liquid down in his lungs."

Archie did a post-mortem, and sure enough, the bird specialist mistakenly drowned the poor crow. That was a sorry lesson for Lizzie.

Archie MacLaughlin raised sheep. One of the problems he had with his sheep was marauding dogs who delighted in chasing the sheep. Rex, in particular, was a big crossbred dog that could catch and kill a lamb just for the fun of it. Archie, an animal lover, was faced with a dilemma. He kept calling the dog's owners, telling them that their dog was killing his sheep and asking them to keep the dog at home. This happened repeatedly.

Archie asked me what I would do if I were in his situation. "Well, Archie, you have been very persistent. You've lost a lot of sheep, and you know we both love animals. That dog will be back, and you have to take care of your sheep." Some time later, I encountered the owner of the dog, who was looking for a new puppy and I asked her how Rex was doing.

"I let him out one day and he never came back."

The next time I was at Archie's, I said, "Archie, I heard that you took care of the problem."

He pointed in the direction of a big oak tree, "You see that tree? Well, he got a proper burial."

Archie had a really old horse that suffered from various ailments and needed to be put down. In the early days, I would actually shoot a horse. It was quick, it was kind, and it was over in a second, but then the euthanizing agents came out, phenobarbital and anesthesia. Administered intravenously, they worked quickly and effectively, and, in fact, so quickly that you had to get out of the way to keep from having the horse topple over on you.

This day, Archie had prepared. He had a backhoe and had dug a proper hole, and we solemnly took the horse to the edge of the hole "Now, Archie," I warned, "this stuff works real fast, so let's not get trapped and have the horse fall on top of us." But before I got one-third of the amount in, the horse suddenly fell into the hole, taking Archie with him. Fortunately, Archie wasn't hurt, just shook up. I had to get a ladder for him so he could climb out of the hole.

Horse Sense

I had been in practice for just a short time when I started getting calls from people with horse farms who also raced horses at Narragansett Park. One of these clients was a chiropodist named John Canzano. John was also a horse trainer and one of the smartest people I ever met. He had a great gift, a photographic memory, and he read textbooks on every subject. We often had long discussions about all kinds of veterinary treatments.

He called me one day from Narragansett Park with a job for me. A man up there had a three-year-old horse that he wanted castrated. I told him I would have to charge $100. (That was a day's pay.)

"Okay. He can pay it."

I arrived promptly, went to the barn, and asked for the owner/trainer.

"Are you the doctor who is going to castrate the killer?" one of the helpers asked me.

"The killer?"

"Oh, yeah. He is a man killer. He needs cutting in the worst way, and I am glad the boss is having him done before he kills somebody."

We castrate horses while they are standing up and backed into the stall. We use an anesthetic so they don't feel any pain, and then maybe we administer something else to calm them down. Normally, I didn't have any problem doing castrations this way, but I thought I'd better have a look at the horse. There was webbing across the front of the stall, and as I looked inside, this great big stud horse came charging at the webbing with his mouth wide open to bite me. I jumped back and he just missed me. He had a wild-looking eye. I thought, "What did I get myself into?"

When the owner/trainer came back, and I asked, "Do you have any good help here?" He told me not to worry. Three men went into the stall, got a chain across the horse's mouth, and backed him into a corner. I had a twitch, or chain, on his nose to restrain him. We were all ready. Another guy came in, so we had four men holding the horse. I loaded my syringe with lidocaine, grabbed his testicle, and touched it with the needle. The horse went absolutely crazy, straight up into the air. The horse took two men, one holding the foot and one holding the twitch, threw them up into the air, wheeled around and kicked one man in the stomach, another man in the leg, then wheeled around again and kicked at me. The man who had been holding the horse's foot went out under the webbing. The horse kicked me, and I flew out under the webbing without a scratch. But the other man who had been tossed out was lying there holding his leg and cursing. His leg was extended under his body as if it were completely detached. Holding onto his leg, he was not only conscious, he was cursing the horse and everybody there. I thought that was pretty remarkable for a man who had just had his leg kicked off. But when he pulled his pantleg up, there was a brand-new cork leg that he had just been fitted for. He was furious.

Needless to say, people came running from all over to see what the commotion was. Now, I had driven all the way up there to castrate this horse, and if I left, I felt it would be a defeat for me; besides, I wanted to make that $100. The trainer asked me, "What do you want to do?"

"The first time, when this horse went up into the air, everybody let go. I need somebody to hold this horse and, no matter what, and not let go."

With that, a tall, muscular man very quietly said to me, "Doctor, do you want me to hold that horse for you?"

"Well, if you don't mind."

"These people here shouldn't be around horses. They don't know the first thing about horses. Let me take hold of him."

So, he spent a little time with the horse. He put a twitch on in his own way and he got that horse to put his head down between his knees. Then, he said, "Go ahead, Doctor."

My hands were shaking, my legs were shaking, and I was very, very reluctant to take another chance, but I didn't have much choice. I went in there, blocked that horse, and castrated him. It took me fifteen minutes and the horse never moved. I learned from that. From then on, if I had anybody helping me hold a horse, it would not be anybody afraid of the horse, because the horse would sense it and somebody could get hurt. Another interesting day in the life of a struggling veterinarian.

Bill Borsay's Guessing Game

Bill Borsay was an English gentleman and a horseman through and through. He was the person who interested me in the Grand Steeplechases and racing in England. Bill had a horse, an old Thoroughbred named Possibility. He had a unique style of training this horse. He would take him into an open field and put him on the end of a lunge line, a thirty-foot line with a snap attached to the halter.

He would crack his whip in the air, and the horse would start galloping around as if he were on a merry-go-round. After he warmed up, Bill would take off the lunge line and simply stand in the middle of the ring and give the horse hand signals and, once in a while, a word of encouragement. Possibility would gallop as if he were training on a racetrack. He would respond to voice commands. Bill would holler, "Whoa," and he would stop. Then Bill would say, "Turn around," sometimes crack his whip, and Possibility would turn around and go back the other way.

This technique served two purposes. Bill was getting the horse fit, and like a person who would be running or jogging or training for a marathon, it preserved the horse's delicate legs. Possibility had suffered multiple problems from his career as a racehorse. But without any weight on his back, Bill could put a foundation under him. Bill's strategy was to get the horse fit on the lunge line, take him to the track, run him in a race, and instruct the jockey that this was his first race in a long time and he didn't want to abuse him. He just wanted him to get a race under his belt, and he'd be riding him the next time. He would get an experienced jockey who would follow his instructions.

Everybody in town knew Bill and Possibility. The game was to figure out when Bill was going to let Possibility run. He maintained an irregular race schedule; he might put over his horse once a year, say, and then, he wouldn't race him for three or four months; the whole process would start over again. People would see him from a distance, and yell, "Possibility?" and Bill would say, "No, no, not yet."

When Bill did run the horse, it was at Narragansett Park, one of the major tracks in the country then. The entire town (there were a lot of people who were interested) would be up there when Bill ran the horse, waiting for Bill to give the word. He always kept them guessing, but those of us who knew his modus operandi would watch Possibility. Every time I would ask, "What do you say, Bill?" he would look around as if people were listening behind the bushes, and then he would whisper, "Today is the day." Possibility never missed. He was a constant source of income.

The Story of Pinetum

The story of Pinetum involves Tommy Gammino, whose father was one of the biggest road builders in the country. Gammino Construction built major highways, not only in Rhode Island but also in other states. I was acquainted with the three boys in the family who worked in the construction business with their father. Tommy and his family lived just up the road from my place in a big old beautiful mansion. Tommy was a good person, kind-hearted, and jovial. And he loved horses.

Many times Tommy would come over here during the day because we had two tracks and trained the horses. There was always something going on. Tommy was just so enamored of it all, the horses and the horse business. He also went to the race-track on occasion; he liked to bet on the horses.

Whenever I ran a horse, Tommy would go to the track; he got all the racing papers, and he knew a little bit about breeding. One day, when I was down at the stable, Tommy said, "Hey, Doc, I want to talk to you. Did you ever hear of a horse named Pinetum?"

"Yes, as a matter of fact, I have. He's racing at Aqueduct and Belmont, the big time. If I'm not mistaken, he's trained by Jim Fitzsimmons." Fitzsimmons was a Hall of Fame trainer, like Wayne Lucas in more recent years.

"Well, I have a chance to get that horse. Would you be inter-ested?"

"How are you going to get a horse like Pinetum?"

"Mike Bove, who has a lot of car dealerships around here, is into racing big time. It happens that we're building a road over in Sakonnet, and we're digging fill and hauling it right past his place on the river. Bove came to the construction site and told me he wanted to build a wall behind his house, and he needed fill. I explained that fill was worth a lot of money, and I asked him if he had any horses he might want to trade. Bove told me that he had a horse with Fitzsimmons, that the horse had hurt a leg and Fitzsimmons was going to have to send him to the farm. Bove was willing to talk to me about trading him."

"Well, I haven't got any place here for a stallion. You can't put a stallion in with the other horses."

Tommy's father had one of the best Holstein farms in the United States; part of his property, Broad Rock Farm, bordered my property. Tommy said, "I'll tell you what, I'll bring my men over here and we'll put up a stallion barn in a day, build it out of cement block, and put a roof on it. I'll clear a piece of land right behind our property, move some trees and boulders, clear it all out for you, and throw a fence up around it." His company could handle something like that.

So I said, "What's the deal, Tommy?"

"I'll build the barn and the paddock. I always wanted to have a horse of my own and we'll be partners. When you find out what's wrong with Pinetum and you straighten him out, we'll take him to the races and we'll win with him. That's all I'm interested in. We'll have some fun."

"Tommy, there's something fishy here. A horse like Pinetum, I mean, there must be something seriously wrong with him. What if you get him up here and I can't fix him?"

"Well, we'll do something with him, send him to an auction or whatever."

I thought I knew Pinetum's breeding; I had the bloodline books, so I said, "Let's go to the house and look in the books and see how this horse is bred."

We found that Pinetum was the son of Me Now out of a really good stake mare. "Well, I don't have anything to lose, Tommy," I said, "but I still think it's a lot of baloney. I don't think you are going to get Pinetum."

Tommy called the next day to say his crew would be here right away, and as soon as the barn and paddock were completed, they were going to ship Pinetum. In the meantime, Tommy would be dropping off the fill at Bove's. Within two or three days, Tommy told me to expect the Lincoln Van Company with Pinetum late in the afternoon.

The van arrived from New York, one of those big twelve-horse vans, with only Pinetum on it. As I signed the bill of lading, the driver said to me, "There is a note here from Mr. Fitzsimmons."

It read, "Look out for this horse. Take extra precaution and have two men handle him when you take him off the truck because he's a man killer."

"Oh, Tommy, I told you there was something fishy."

Among the spectators was one of Tommy's close friends, a state trooper named Jim Ahearn. Jim was also a horse lover who ended up training horses. He used to have the horses swim in the ocean for exercise. Jim Ahearn was a big, rugged guy; he could handle any horse. I showed him the note and he said, "Well, you give me one shank and you take the other and we'll get this horse out of the van." Inside the van, we saw a magnificent chestnut stallion. As soon as we approached him—he was chained on both sides—he tried to rear up and opened his mouth as if he was going to bite. I said, "Well, I've seen bad horses before; he can't be that bad." We put the shanks on him and he came bouncing off that trailer and dragged us up to the new stallion barn.

Tommy opened up the barn and it took all we had to handle Pinetum. We got him in the stall and closed the door. The three of us stood outside the stall door, and I said, "Well, Tommy, looks like we got something here. I don't know what we are going to do with him or how we'll handle him."

"You can handle him."

"Well then, let's see how bad he really is."

The stall door was a heavy double door with strong latches top and bottom. When we opened the upper door, Pinetum came screaming at us, his mouth open. We jumped back; he just missed us. He wheeled around and let both hind feet go, almost kicking the door down. I said, "We've got to condition this horse to behave and I've got to master him."

"How are you going to do that?"

"Watch."

I walked around the back of the barn where I had some tools. I picked up a broken axe handle and said to Jim Ahearn, "I'm going in there to catch him. When he comes at me, I'll swing this ax handle and hit him between his ears. I will do it because it's either him or me. Open it just enough for me to squeeze about halfway through in case I have to come out. If I can't get him under control, you've got to be behind me."

Pinetum was over in the corner of the stall, and as soon as we opened the stall door, he came at me, eyes full of fire, mouth open, with a little foam in his mouth, and a wild look. I hit him right between the eyes. That's an old expression called "poleaxing." Pinetum was dazed and went down.

I know that sounds cruel, and I'll probably get a lot of flack for it, but this kind of treatment is sometimes necessary. Pinetum struggled to his feet, dizzy and dazed, and backed up in the stall. I stood there with the ax handle, and he just stood in the corner. He looked at me and I looked at him. We stood there for what must have been five minutes, and then I pointed the ax handle and said to him, "Get over here." I started to inch toward him, and sure enough, he moved over. Jim handed me the shank, and with the ax handle in one hand and the shank in the other, I walked up to the horse. I paraded him around the stall, took him out, put him back in the stall, closed the door, and I said, "Now, let's see what happens."

Pinetum turned out to be a perfect gentleman. From that beginning and after his racing days were over, I bred a lot of mares by myself here with him. The barn stood for a long time with his brass tack on the door. We have oil paintings of Pinetum that people did. He was just a great horse. He wouldn't do anything unless I told him it was okay.

We started to train Pinetum. First, I took care of his leg problem, which involved a tendon. I had had good luck treating tendons; I put some heat blisters on him to stimulate the blood flow, and the healing began with no problem. After about two months, Martha Watson started to gallop him. After he had trained for a month or so, he was just too much for her to handle. I remembered "Virginia" Robertson, and I went to see him, to tell him we would like him to train Pinetum. "If we can get this horse sound and up to racing, I believe he is going to be a good horse and we ought to be able to win with him." Robertson started training him, and it wasn't long before he called me to say, "Doc, this is a racehorse. This horse can run. There isn't anything up here that can beat him. I've handled a lot of horses, as you know, and I know a runner when I see one. This horse is a runner."

Since Tommy didn't know much about horses and training, I warned Robertson, "Don't tell Tommy too much because he has a lot of friends. If he has the chance, he'll tell all his friends and they'll all be at the track; we'll have to bet two dollars to make two dollars. We need to be careful about not letting the word out."

Robertson had his own jockey, Ronnie Fisher, who rode exclusively for him. He was deliberately working Pinetum slowly, so that the clockers at the track wouldn't get an idea of how fast he was. The time came when Robertson said, "Doc, this horse is ready." He entered Pinetum in a race. At that point, there were no statistics on him; nobody knew anything about him. Tommy was excited and wanted to know what Robertson said. I told him that he was probably going to try Pinetum in a couple of races just to look over the competition.

Tommy drove me to the track and walked over to the stable to see Pinetum before he was taken to the paddock for the race. Pinetum had just been washed and he was shivering. That's an indication that a horse is really ready.

Tommy asked, "Why is he shaking?"

"He's nervous Tommy."

Robertson got me on the side and said, "Doc, this is like stealing candy from a baby. What did you tell Tommy?"

I said, "We won't tell him anything until the last minute."

People would come to see the horses saddled before the race. To many race goers, that was part of the fun of racing, to see the horses and what they looked like and what condition they were in. There must have been fifty people in front of Pinetum's stall. They looked like the Gammino construction gang. I said, "You know, Tommy, Virginia still hasn't told me whether he'll let Pinetum run today, because if he lets him run and he's not ready, he might hurt himself."

As we left the paddock for the grandstand, the horses went to the track. As we walked, Tommy's gang walked behind us, waiting to get the word from him.

"Tommy, you remind me of the Pied Piper of Hamelin."

"Who's that?"

I told him the fable about a man who was hired to get rid of all the rats in town. He played the flute and all the rats followed him into the sea and drowned. Tommy didn't appreciate that, but we went up to the box to watch the race. Tommy had brought a roll of money with him to bet.

"When are you going to tell me so I can bet?"

"Well, we've arranged with Ronnie Fisher that when he gets behind the gate and it's one minute to post, he's going to raise up in the irons if everything is okay."

"Geez, I won't have time to bet," he complained.

"No, and neither will your friends. That's the way we have to do it. Virginia and I worked all this out."

In the meantime, those of us in the know had placed our bets.

"Look, Tommy, Ronnie raised up to go."

Tommy ran out of the box, down the steps to the betting window, tripped and ripped his pants, but got to the window just in time to tell the clerk, "Start punching till I tell you to stop." Tommy got to put $500 on Pinetum. When the bell rang, the horses took off. Pinetum just galloped. There was no contest. He paid a pretty good price and Tommy cashed in. He was too excited to drive his car home.

Two weeks later, we ran Pinetum again and he won again, this time against better horses. Then, a couple of weeks later, the tendon started to swell up again, and we decided that he was too nice a horse and we didn't want to hurt him. So we brought him home and he spent four or five years as a stallion, siring some nice horses.

When I first met Tommy, everybody called him "Moose." I called him Tommy. I never was comfortable calling him Moose because I didn't know how he got the nickname. When I got to know him better, I asked him, "I'm curious, Tommy, why do they call you Moose?"

"Oh, you don't know about that?"

He told me he was a pretty good football player in prep school and he, like every Catholic athlete in the United States, wanted to go to Notre Dame. I'm not sure if Rockne or Leahy was the coach, but, in any case, they had a squad of God knows how many of the best prep school players. They would win by scores like sixty-two to nothing. Whenever a game was a runaway, the coach would let everybody on the squad get in the game, and that way, they could always say afterwards that they played for Notre Dame.

I suspect that was the case with Tommy. He said he reported along with hundreds of others for practice. One of the first things they did was to run down under punts, so he was determined to show his stuff. When one guy punted downfield, Tommy was going full speed, and just as the receiver caught the ball, Tommy ran into him and the ball flew out of his hands. The receiver was on the ground and didn't come to for about five minutes. After they finally revived him, he was still all shook up and dazed. Finally he said, "What hit me, a moose?"

A Question of Ethics

Not all of my clients were honest. One in particular did a couple of things that disturbed me. I had a client who kept Guernsey cows in Bristol, Rhode Island, and I would make a weekly trip to Bristol to work on his herd. He was looking for another place, and I mentioned the Sturges estate, which I understood was for sale. He didn't waste any time. He moved into the house along with his new wife and her favorite pug dog.

The Pug Dog

Pug dogs make a funny noise, almost a snoring sound because of the conformation of their little heads; they have short noses and short palates. They are cute little dogs and were very popular at that time.

One night, this client shows up at my place and says, "Doctor, I want to ask you a favor. Do you have anything that you could give a dog to put him to sleep?"

What do you mean, put him to sleep?

"You know. I want this dog to go to sleep and not wake up."

"What are you talking about?"

"Well, look, I'm going to tell you something, just between me and you. My wife insists on taking this little dog to bed with her. It keeps me up all night moving around and snoring. We get into real battles over this dog. I do not want it sleeping in my bed at night. I think that if she had to choose between me and the dog, she'd choose the dog

"I'm not going to have anything to do with something like that."

"Well, I thought I'd ask you."

He was always kidding and joking, and I didn't know whether he was serious. At any rate, he left here, and I thought that was the end of it.

About a week later, I got a call early in the morning from his wife, who was hysterical; she had awakened to find that her little dog was dead. At least, she thought he was, and she wanted me to come right over. I hurried across the road. She was crying and the husband was there, all teary eyed and shaking his head, saying he didn't know what could have happened to such a young dog. I went through the motions of trying to detect a pulse, while the husband had his arm around his wife and was putting on quite a show. When I looked at him, there was a glint in his eye that sent me a signal that said, "You had better not say anything." Well, I couldn't prove what had happened, but I was pretty sure I knew.

The Belgian Horses

Another time, this same client talked to me about getting a team of horses. He had a notion that he would like to participate in pulling contests at the local fairs. He was willing to pay a lot of money for a good pair. I told him, "All the people around here go down to Lancaster, Pennsylvania, to the Amish country, where they have a big auction."

He sent a representative with instructions to buy a team of Belgian horses. His agent paid a lot of money for a beautiful matched team and he bought the harnesses. They brought the team back, and he took lessons; he would stand behind the team with the long reins and drive them up and down the field. He decided that he was going to add carriages and wagons, and drive them in parades. Pretty soon he had a beautiful wagon with a little hand brake, a miniature of the Budweiser wagons.

The first day that the horses were hitched up, he sat behind them, slapped the reins, and off they went. They started slowly and gradually began to run. He applied the brake but soon he was yelling, "Whoa." The horses went faster. They ran all over the whole place, including some rocks, which damaged the wagon. He was lucky to escape with his life.

He said, "I need a professional to tell me what's wrong with these horses." Someone came, fixed the wagon, locked the wheels, put weights in the back, and trained the horses, who apparently were green. Then he loaded the wagon, put double brakes on each wheel, and had each wheel locked and chained. "Now," he said, "we'll see what happens." When he started up, again the team started slowly, dragging the wagon, and then started to take off. The professional said, "I've never seen runaways like this. That must be why they sold them."

So my client decided to get rid of these horses. He sent word around that he had a beautiful team of horses for sale. There was an order of contemplative monks in Cumberland, Rhode Island, north of here. They had a very fine Holstein dairy herd that had been given to them by the elder Michael Gammino. This monastic order was bound by a vow of silence, but one of the monks would have permission to speak when there was business to be done. When the monk asked the reason for selling, he was told that the owner just got tired of them. The monks couldn't understand why this handsome team and all the beautiful equipment was for sale. They haggled about the price and finally arrived at a very low figure. I wish I could have been there when they hitched up that team to the wagon. I'll bet they broke their vow of silence that day.

No Pay Charlie

My practice, a farm practice, was growing by leaps and bounds, and it was becoming increasingly difficult for me to get to the racetrack. I would go only on special occasions or when somebody would call me for a consultation. Charlie Hernandez was one of the people who asked me if I would look at a horse for him, which I did. He had left his family in Cuba to come here with a couple of horses. He was trying to make enough money to send to his family in Cuba. After I finished treating his horse, he told me he didn't have any money right then, but he would see that I got paid.

On the way out, I bumped into one of the regular track veterinarians, Dr. Ed Cole. We were at the University of Pennsylvania at the same time.

"I see you were treating a horse for No Pay Charlie."

"No Pay Charlie?"

"Oh, Charlie doesn't have any money. He does the same thing to everybody, so we nicknamed him No Pay Charlie."

Charlie started to win some races, and suddenly was doing very well. Furthermore, Charlie was what you call a betting trainer. He had friends who would bet for him. He wore spats and had a little mustache and always had a big Cuban cigar in his mouth—he was a real character. When he began doing well, he sent for his family. They all enjoyed South County and we became friends.

Subsequently, I gave him a couple of horses to train. But then, Charlie started to fall on hard times. I guess a couple of his bets went awry. He had arranged to ship his horses to Florida, because up north in winter, the racetracks were closed. Before they left, I had to go to Narragansett Park to look at a horse.

As I drove through the guard gate, Charlie jumped in front of my car, waving his arms wildly. I stopped the car and he ran over.

"Doctor, Doctor, I'm so glad to see you. I'm in big trouble. I need to ship out, and I don't have enough money to pay the van man. Can you lend me some money?"

"How much do you need, Charlie?"

"How much have you got?"

I took out my wallet, and counted out about $200 while he watched.

"Doctor, if you can lend me $200, you'll save my life. I'll send you the money when I get down there. I got a couple of horses. I'm going to win some races down there, and you can trust me.

Besides, when I have a horse that runs, I'll call you. Maybe you can bet with a bookmaker

"Fine, Charlie. That's okay, I trust you."

Charlie took off. I followed Charlie's activity in the newspaper to see how he was doing. I never saw that he won a race, and I never heard from him all winter.

Then, the following spring, racing started here again. My wife and I used to go to Suffolk Downs on Wednesday afternoons. There were beautiful dining rooms, and we'd ride the elevator up to the Turf Club. That day, as my wife and I were approaching the elevator, we noticed, over on the side, a group of people gathered around Charlie Hernandez.

The man running the elevator told me, "Charlie put over a horse up here and he's done well. He's in the money."

"I can't believe he didn't call me." I was getting madder by the second.

My wife suggested, "Maybe there's a reason. Why don't you go talk to him?"

"That's what I'm going to do. I won't be long."

When Charlie spied me, he threw his arms around me, and started hugging me, asking about my family.

"Never mind that, Charlie, the elevator man told me that you made a big score."

With that, he stepped back and looked at me. He reached into his jacket pocket and pulled out a knife, one of those snap knives with a blade that pops out. He put the knife in my hand.

"Doctor, what you just done to me, you might as well kill me. Go ahead, if that's what you think, that I made a score and I didn't call you. It's just like you stabbed me."

"Geez, Charlie, I'm just telling you what the man said."

"You would believe him? I've been embarrassed. I didn't call you because I didn't have the money, and I wasn't doing good."

"Okay, Charlie. I'm sorry. My wife is waiting for me. I've gotta go."

My wife asked me how it went, and I told her the story. And I said, "I had four or five hundred dollars in my pocket, and I think I'm pretty lucky because in another five minutes Charlie would have had that, too."

Charlie had a friend named Emilio Rodriguez, who was then a successful jockey and later a very successful trainer. He came from Cuba about the same time Charlie did. When I recounted that story to Emilio, he said, "That's Charlie. In Cuba, he was known as the world's greatest actor."

Investigating an Insurance Claim

I received a call from an insurance company representative in San Francisco asking me if I would be willing to go across the Bay to Newport. He got my name from the dean of the veterinary school at Colorado State University. The insurance man wanted to know if I'd check on a case that involved a very valuable horse that was insured for $50,000.

The horse in question had been leased to a woman in Fairfield, Connecticut, for her daughter. Part of the agreement was that she would take out an insurance policy. It appeared that the horse had taken a few bad steps. A cyst was found in the navicular bone in its foot. I studied the X-rays from the veterinarian in Connecticut. It was a common finding, not necessarily life-threatening and not necessarily destroying the usefulness of the horse. I had seen many such cysts that were just artifacts.

I visited the woman and told her that I represented the insurance company, that I was following up on her claim. She brought out a bay mare, ten years old, for me to look at and I said that I'd like to see the horse move. She said that the horse had been shod with a special type of shoe, that it was lame and couldn't be used, that they were going to have to put her down. I didn't think the horse was lame, but I went through the routine of looking at it. Something was off here. The mare matched the description; the color, sex, and age were right, but just didn't look to me like a valuable open jumper. I told the woman that

I'd need to file a report. When I got home, I called the insurance company and said that there was a real possibility that this horse was not the one that was insured, that I wanted to go back, unannounced, to find out if my suspicions were correct. The insurance company agreed.

The woman had told me that if I needed to come back, I would not be able to reach her in the mornings between 8:30 and 10 o'clock, because that is when she did her errands. Naturally, I chose that very time for my return visit. A young woman greeted me and took me way back in the barn, to a big stall where there was a gorgeous animal that was obviously not the horse I had looked at.

I went out and waited. When the woman returned, she said, "Oh, Dr. Kaplan, I didn't expect you."

"No, I guess you didn't. I've just seen the horse that I was supposed to look at, and apparently you are trying to defraud the insurance company."

She looked at me very downhearted and said, "We've been having trouble. Can we talk about it?"

I turned away and got into the car. When I got back to the office, I called the insurance company, and reported my discovery. I had heard of scams involving people who would do something like that to an animal, just for insurance purposes. I was really amazed that such a thing went on.

High Finance

When I first bought my property, we were surrounded by farms. Across the road was a large farm named Shadblow, with a herd of purebred cows. The owner was Melvin Sawin, a New York stockbroker. Hans Hess and his wife were the tenants; they were general caretakers and excellent farmers. Whenever I did any work at Shadblow, I had to send the bills to Sawin's New York office. I would send monthly statements to New York, and he would take many months before paying something on the bill. If he owed me $200, he might send me $40, or if he owed me $300, he might send me $100. He always ran a balance with everybody, whether it was the Wakefield Branch, which delivered oil, or the plumber, or any of the local tradespeople who sent him bills. Sawin used other people's money for his investments—a pretty clever trick, if you can get away with it. He was always adding to the balance, so I had no chance of ever catching up, and I resented it because I'm not a very good bookkeeper, and I felt it was unfair.

Sawin used to come up from New York on the weekends and go out to the barn and talk with Hans. There was income from the cows, from selling a little milk. People would come over with their milk cans. Hans sold the milk and recorded the amount, and Sawin would report it as income. In addition, I also suspected that he used his big estate as a business write-off.

One particular weekend, Hans called to say that a cow was trying to calve and he and his wife hadn't been able to help her. Being right across the road, I hurried over and delivered the calf without too much trouble and then washed up. For something like this, my routine was that I would strip to the waist and fill a bucket with warm water and add disinfectant and then soap myself up. I was just taking my coveralls off when Mr. Sawin came into the barn. He was a big, aristocratic-looking guy and thought he was something special.

"Well, Doctor, what are you doing over here on a Sunday?"

"This cow had a little trouble calving."

"Is everything all right?"

"Oh, yeah. Everything's fine."

"Well, that's good. Nice to see you."

And as he turned away to go back to the big house, I called after him, "Mr. Sawin, do you get my bills down at your New York office?"

"Oh, I expect so. I never look at the bills; my secretary takes care of it. Why? Haven't you been getting paid?"

"Oh, I've been getting paid, Mr. Sawin, but every month it's a small fraction instead of the full amount, and the outstanding balance keeps getting bigger. I really don't mind, but I thought I'd tell you I'm charging you 100 percent interest. I just wondered if you knew that."

"Would you mind explaining that?"

"Sure, Mr. Sawin. Normally, for what I did today, I would charge you $25, but when I get home I'll write $50 in my book. I figure that you're using my money by never paying the bill in full, so I'll just turn it around. I don't know how much interest you make on my money, but I figure 100 percent interest is fair enough."

He stopped for a moment, looked at me and Hans and then he said, "Hans, from now on when the doctor comes here for anything, you pay him out of petty cash."

With that, Sawin turned and stormed out of the barn. As soon as he was out the door, Hans and I threw our arms around each other, laughing.

Hans said, "I thought the old man was going to have a heart attack. You really put it to him. He deserved it. He does that with everybody. I call to get equipment fixed and I'm told they'll do it when Sawin pays his bill in full. I'll never have enough money in that jar to pay you. Just keep sending the bills."

"Well, he might fire me, Hans. He might tell you to get some-body else."

"Well, if he does, he'd better fire me, too."

That went on for quite a while. I continued to double my bill, and Sawin continued to allow the bill to run up, but I figured I got even with him eventually.

Another Gentleman Farmer

Another man, also a New York stockbroker, lived on the Commodore Perry Farm, a historic farm purchased in 1814 by Admiral Perry (who coined the phrase, "We have met the enemy and they are ours"). This fellow's name was Wisner Townsend, and he raised various animals, mainly sheep. He acquired a large flock and was a very concerned owner. Whenever the sheep didn't look right, he would call me. He was a fine gentleman, a good conversationalist, and had a great sense of humor. He liked to talk about his many experiences and mostly about the stock market.

He wasn't making a living from the farming certainly, but, again, he was another one who, I figured out later on, was using the farm as a tax gimmick. However, he paid his bills promptly and he was a good client. I went there for quite a long time.

One noontime I was over there taking care of the sheep. Wisner's wife had gone somewhere but she had left him something to eat. He asked me to have lunch with him and we could talk. I didn't have too busy a day and I thought that would be a grand idea. So, we went up to the house, had a sandwich and a beer and some cake, and we exchanged our stories, as usual.

Finally, I looked at my watch and said, "I've spent too much time already, and I think I'd better be going."

"Oh, wait a minute. How much do I owe you? I'll pay you right here."

"Oh, that's okay, Wisner. I'll send you a bill at the end of the month."

"No. I'll pay you now. Save you sending a bill."

From that point on, for probably the next year, he paid me before I left. Then one time I went there to take care of what he thought was a major problem. Afterwards, he invited me up to the house and said he'd pay me and we'd have a bite to eat. He sat there looking at me with a funny expression on his face.

"You know, I figured it all out. I looked at all the old bills. There's a twenty percent difference between what you used to charge when you sent the bills and what you charge me when I pay you at the door."

"Now, Wisner, I don't think so. Why would that be?"

"I know why it would be. When you're at home making out bills, you've got a lot more nerve with that pencil than you do when you're here looking me in the eye. That's how it is."

I started laughing, and said, "I wouldn't have believed it."

"Well, you'd better believe it. I got the records right here to prove it," said he.

Never Judge a Book by Its Cover

A stranger came to my office with some sick cats. He told me that a friend of his had recommended me. The cats had a respiratory disease. I wasn't entirely sure what it was, but by that time we had antibiotics to treat a lot of these infections successfully.

The man was driving a truck that should have been in the junkyard. It was all rusted, it had no hubcaps, and the springs on the seats were all showing. He was wearing work clothes. Obviously, he didn't have much money. I finished injecting the cats, and I had to give him some medicine to take home. He wanted to know how much he owed. Because I perceived him to be a very poor man, I charged him only a couple of dollars, which didn't even cover the cost of the medicine. He looked very surprised and said, "Well, that is very reasonable," as he paid me. It turned out that he had a dozen cats at his place, and there was always something wrong with one cat or another. For the next year, he continued to be a steady client and I continued to charge him little or nothing because he seemed to be such a good person and he loved his cats so much.

Then one day I got a call from his wife. She was in a panic; one of their favorite Siamese cats was having a convulsion. She said her husband was on the way home from work and wondered if he could come to the office. I said, "Sure. You tell him to come." Soon, a black Mercedes drove in. It was a beauty, the most expensive new model.

This time he was dressed in a three-piece suit, Gucci shoes and all. I asked, "Where is your old car?"

"Oh, the only time I ever use that car is to take the cats to the vet."

"That's a good one. I've been thinking all along that you were a pauper."

"Well, I thought you *were* pretty reasonable."

Needless to say, the next time he came in, I put it right to him and I haven't seen him since.

Ask the Veterinarian

The sea wall in Narragansett borders the ocean, and during a storm the tide can sweep over the wall and onto the main road, Ocean Road. This wall is a great source of pride and beauty, and people take advantage of walking there. I walk there daily. I look forward to seeing the people. I know just about everybody by sight. We say hello while we're walking even though we might not know who we're saying hello to!

There is one particular group of resident experts: Jane and Don Heskith, both retired teachers; Jerry McVicker and his wife Dolores; Ernie Hogan, whose health is getting better according to our frequent phone conversations; Bob Miller, an outstanding athlete and coach (a lot of people call him "Coach"), and Bob can hold his own when it comes to story telling, but he has

90th birthday breakfast, left to right: Mike Rogers, Ernie Hogan, George Malgieri, Doc, and John Avella

met his match in this group; George Malgieri, postmaster for a long time in Narragansett; John Avella, a retired Providence businessman; Mike Rogers, an expert on UFOs, with all kinds of pictures to prove that there is extraterrestrial life out there; and Warren and Millie Whittier, former members of our group.

One summer day, there was a heated discussion: one of us claimed he had seen a mink running across the rocks on the sea side of the wall.

He was immediately challenged, "I never saw a mink down there. It was probably a big rat."

Another one contributed, "You can tell the difference between a rat and a mink by the tail."

Yet another chipped in, "Maybe it was a beaver."

Then it dawned on someone to ask the veterinarian. I had listened to it all, so I said, "I'll tell you how you know. What color were its eyes?" That set off a big laugh. We've been kidding ever since.

The sea wall is a great place to meet. We don't discuss our ailments or infirmities. We think positive. This is a vital part of life in Narragansett.

My Young Colleagues

When I think about of all I've done and seen since I graduated from veterinary school, there are so many things that I feel proud of, that I feel privileged to have been able to do. What has given me the most pleasure has been helping many young people to pursue their professional careers. I can count so many young men and women I have helped along the way, advising, helping them financially, guiding them, encouraging them. They have gone on to jobs including state veterinarian, reproductive veterinarian, head of department at the University of Pennsylvania, and head of a large equine organization, to name a few.

Melissa Mckendry

One young woman of whom I am very proud is Melissa Mckendry. I met her after she had completed one year of veterinary school in the Bahamas and convinced her to apply to an accredited school in this country. She got her degree from the University of Tennessee and now practices in Virginia Beach, Virginia. Melissa is a generous person. In addition to her practice, she runs an animal shelter there and provides services not normally offered at animal shelters—surgery, ultrasound, amputations, prosthetics, to name a few. I am regularly in touch with Melissa. I've met her husband, a Navy Seal, and her two children.

She wanted to contribute the following to this book:

Dr. Martin Kaplan has been the fundamental positive influence in not only my professional but personal life. Over the years, his stories have taught me lessons that have guided me in many difficult decisions. Doc has helped, through inspiration and support, many aspiring veterinarians. I hope to continue to follow in his path as an accomplished veteri-narian and giving individual.

Melissa Mckendry with Max and Lily in 2007

On my Saturday rounds, my station wagon would often be full of young people who helped at the farm; many were veterinary students. After each call, we would discuss the case as we drove around, and we really had an enjoyable time. It was a good learning experience for those young people. Today, four of those students are practicing in Rhode Island, and quite often they talk about those days when they rode with me and how much fun it was. I feel that is what it's all about for me. I still keep in touch with these young people. I get telephone calls, cards, and letters from them from time to time.

Willard "Mike" Freeman

After I had bought my first few Thoroughbred horses, a young man came by and introduced himself as Willard "Mike" Freeman. His father had hopes for Mike as a businessman, but Mike thought differently. He loved horses and he could ride. He was a University of Rhode Island student, and he asked if I had any horses I wanted trained or galloped, that he'd like to have a job. I realized how valuable he might be. So, he became one of the young men who trained for me.

After Mike graduated, he started in training for himself. I gave him some of the first horses he trained while he was in New England, but he was such a good trainer that he soon became well known and he moved to Maryland. He married there and I was an usher at his wedding. Mike went on to become a prominent trainer. He trained for Alfred Vanderbilt, who owned Native Dancer.

I had a very nice mare here, Eternal Mark. She was good enough that she had run out of competition locally, so I wanted to send her to the big tracks, where the prize money was far better than here in New England, and where we could get some recognition in the horse-racing industry. Mike Freeman was then in New York, and I called him to ask if he knew any trainers there that I could send her to.

"How about me? I'll take Eternal Mark for you."

"But you're training for C.V. Whitney. Are you sure?"

"Yes. I have an agreement with Mr. Whitney that I can occasionally take an outside horse." Well, that was great and I sent the horse to Mike.

In a week or so, he called me and said, "This mare, she's good. She doesn't like anybody in front of her and she has a great deal of ability. There's a race in the condition book that I think will fit her very well." The condition book was issued a week or ten days in advance of a race by the racing secretary so that you could pick races that were well suited to your horse.

"And now, as far as a jockey goes," he said, "I can get Willie

Shoemaker to ride her." Willie Shoemaker, even then, was probably one of the ten best jockeys in racing history.

After Mike called me, my wife and I made reservations at the Taft Hotel, where Guy Lombardo used to play. We'd go to New York once a month, see the plays and the musical productions on Broadway, and always stay at the Taft. That was part of our routine and we enjoyed it.

Anyhow, we were in the paddock for Eternal Mark's first race, and I told Shoemaker (you couldn't call him Willie, Mike had told me), "Bill, this mare has never been beaten. She comes out of the gate and goes to the front. She's had ten races around New England for me, and she's won them all. I've run her at the different tracks, never the big time, but there's one thing you want to remember. Just don't stand up on her. If she doesn't break in front, if she gets behind, just be patient and she'll work herself out of there and she'll get to the front." Being a New England horse, the comment of the handicapper was "good in New England."

At the start of the race, Eternal Mark went right to the front and opened up many lengths around the turn. She won it so easily that right away Mike Freeman said, "We'd better start looking for some good stake races for this mare." And that's what happened. She won at six different race tracks, all the Maryland tracks. I then felt I had really gotten into the big time. Eternal Mark was featured on the front page of the racing form, which all the people in racing read.

Mike eventually trained a filly named Shuvee, who won the Triple Crown. After winning the Triple Crown, Mike and his wife, who was from a racing family, established their own training center in Aiken, South Carolina. Years later, some local Rhode Island people sent their horses down to Aiken for the winter, and they were surprised when Mike asked them about me, what I was doing. They had no idea of that early relationship between me and Mike. It shows just how much fun it was to be in racing and experience that kind of success.

John Barrett

John Barrett, a graduate of URI, was working as a paramedic. He came to me one day and asked if he could start riding around with me because he had always wanted to be a veterinarian. He was getting close to thirty years old and was not satisfied with his career. He looked to me as if he might be a likely candidate for veterinary school. He started to ride with me and we talked about veterinary medicine. I found him to be extremely intelligent and well motivated. But during our conversations, he admitted to one drawback: in his college days, he had studied just enough to get by, had not even begun to live up to his God-given talents. He was concerned that any admissions committee looking at his undergraduate record would not consider him.

After much discussion, I called Dr. Vance Yates, chairman of the pathology department at URI, a veterinarian and noted authority on many diseases, principally poultry diseases. He and another friend of mine, Dr. Huie Chang, had developed an international reputation. Dr. Yates gave a graduate course in pathology, and he knew John's family because they lived in Kingston. He said that he had an opening in his pathology class, but it was very difficult and he didn't want to waste his time, or the

Poultry faculty, Huie Chang back row left, Vance Yates middle row right

class's either, by admitting someone who couldn't do the work. So he said, "I'll admit him in the first semester, but not only will he have to be able to pass, he must also have enough motivation to earn a grade of A." John accepted the challenge. He enrolled in Dr. Yates's course, and sure enough, he did A work. Dr. Yates told me that John was an excellent student.

After completing that course, John applied to various veterinary schools in the country. They looked at his undergraduate record, and, unfortunately, because the competition was so stiff, he was rejected on that basis alone. He was advised to take further courses and if he continued to do excellent work he might be reconsidered. John took the advice and for the next year; he took courses and excelled, but that big stumbling block was still there. Veterinary colleges, of which there were relatively few, were taking only students with the best undergraduate records. John became discouraged. I continued to keep after him.

One day, he came to my office and said, "Doc, are you going to be disappointed in me? I've just been accepted to medical school, and I'm thinking about it because I just don't know how long it's going to be before I'll ever get admitted to veterinary school."

"John, although it's not veterinary medicine, it is medicine, and I think you will make a fine doctor." So John went off to medical school, and, of course, we kept in touch.

While he was in medical school, he left his Siberian Husky dog, which he loved dearly, with his mother in Kingston. His mother brought the dog to the office for various ailments and vaccinations. From the very beginning, when she offered to pay me for my services, I told her that John and I had an agreement: I was going to take care of his dog while he was in medical school, and after he graduated, he would take care of me for the rest of my life, as long as it takes, and not going to charge me. What are the chances of that happening?

The dog lived a long, active life, and later on had multiple problems. I continued to take care of him. It took quite a while for John to finish medical school and serve his internship. And what do you think happened? John came back, got connected with another doctor in Wakefield, opened up his practice, and I became one of his first patients. It's been several years since John started practicing. Now I am kidding him about which one of us is getting the better part of the deal.

John Canty

One day, a young man showed up here on a bicycle asking for me. He had such a thick Irish brogue, I could hardly understand him. Someone had referred him, and he started riding around with me. After he'd been here a short time and I got to know him, I found out he had only a temporary visa, and the time came when he had to go back to Ireland. He was hoping that he could stay here. There were too many veterinarians in Ireland, so there was little opportunity for employment, and he had a girlfriend here.

I called Senator Chafee in Washington and told him that my Irish cousin, a veterinarian, had a visitor's visa that was about to expire. Senator Chafee got John an extension for one year. I called Dick DeStasio, a trainer in New York, to see if his track veterinarian could use any help. John got the job, went off in his beat-up old truck to New York, and worked at the racetrack there.

At the end of a year, his visa was about to expire. Not wanting to impose on me again, he hired one of those "specialists" in immigrant visas, the ones who take your money and don't do anything for you. At the last minute, he called me with only forty-eight hours left before he had to go back. I got in touch with Senator Chafee, who straightened things out for us again. Within a year or two, John Canty had his green card and he married the young woman he had been going with. He didn't want anyone to think that he married her so he could stay here. Now John has four lovely children (one of them with the middle name of Kaplan), and his wife graduated from the University of Florida Veterinary School. Nothing gives me more satisfaction than doing something like that for these two.

Severence MacLaughlin

Severence is the grandchild of Archie MacLaughlin, the man who trained the crow to speak. As a high school senior, Severence was an outstanding student and my assistant. Wherever I took him on calls with me, people remarked afterwards, "Who was that nice young man you had with you?" His manners were impeccable, his study habits were the same, and in a large high school class, he finished fifth.

I teased him, "There's room for improvement."

"Well, those other kids were pretty tough to beat."

Severence rode around with me on Saturdays. He came from a small farm and won the 4H award at the Washington County Fair for being an outstanding sheep herdsman. He understood all kinds of animals. As we made our calls, I suggested that he take notes of our observations to prepare him for college. During the first six months or so that he went around with me, I would quiz him; he'd say that he had written it down, but then he'd kind of stumble around. I would tell him, "You know, Severence, you've got to write all this down. It's very important now because you'll remember it." There was no question in my mind that he would be able to go to just about any veterinary school he wanted.

One Saturday, we had quite a few calls on our schedule. At the first stop, my wife had left a message that Marguerite Lensner had a sick horse. It was on the way, so we set out for her little farm in the middle of nowhere. As we were driving, I would tell Severence about my clients and how to handle things, how we would need to use a little psychology and judgment. This time I said, "Now, this farm is not a fancy farm, but I've known this woman for a very long time, and she loves animals and she would do without so that her animals would have enough to eat. And another thing, when we finish treating the animal, she's going to say to me, 'I don't have any money right now, but I'll be up next week to pay you.' That is how she is and that'll be okay."

We walked into the barn, and I smelled a very strange smell. I asked, "What is that smell, Marguerite?"

"Turpentine. I mixed turpentine with milk, half and half, and put it down the horse and tried to get her stomach working the way it says in my old book."

"Well, let's see what we can do." So, we figured out what the problem was, treated the horse, and finished up.

"I certainly appreciate your coming," she said."I don't have any money right now, but I'll be up."

Severence did his best to keep from laughing. When we got to the car, he said, "That was amazing, that was just word for word."

"I've heard it so often I know the spiel. She's a good person, and she'll never catch up to what she owes me, but she'll always pay me on account." It's that kind of person who has been the backbone of my practice from way back.

In 2006, Severence MacLaughlin submitted his doctoral thesis to the University of Adelaide, Australia. The thesis was entitled, "The Impact of the Periconceptional Environment (in vivo and ex vivo) on Feto-Placental Development in the Sheep," and I was proud to see my name listed among the people he acknowledged:

> *Dr. Martin O. Kaplan, Thank you for taking an interest in me during my youth. Your guidance and encouragement allowed me to fulfill my dream. It does not seem that long ago that I was riding with you. Thank you, you are like a grandfather to me.*

He sent us his bound thesis with this inscription:

> *Thank you so much for providing me a foundation for my education, mentoring me, and helping me achieve my dreams. Your support through the years has meant a great deal to me. Much love, Severence*

Earlier, he had written to us:

Dear Dr. and Mrs. Kaplan,

I must apologize for the tardiness of this note. Thank you very much for the gifts that you gave me in September and December [2004]. It made life easier and I am very thankful. However, I am more thankful for the knowledge and love that you have shared with me over the years. Doc, you are a model person and I hope I can touch people's lives as you have. Thank you. Much love, Severence

Mike Bruzzi

Of all the young people that I've helped, I am so proud of a young man named Michael Bruzzi. Mike came here as a smart, know-it-all kid from the city. While he was a student at URI, he showed up here one day with another student, a pretty girl. They both were in pre-veterinary medicine. The girl wanted to know if there was any chance that they could go on calls with me. I said, "Sure. You be here Saturday morning, and you can ride with me." As Mike tells the story, they had planned it that way. He figured that they would have a better chance of success if the girl did the asking.

Michael Bruzzi ended up living here. We gave him a little room down at the stable, and in exchange for his room, he took care of the horses and did a lot of chores. On a farm there is always something to do, and it turned out that Michael was very handy. His one problem was that he was always in too much of a hurry to get things done.

While he was with us, my wife, an outstanding cook who took great delight in preparing evening meals fit for a king, insisted that Mike have dinner with us every night. While he was away at school, she would go down to the barn and collect all his dirty clothes to wash and iron. Pretty soon, Mike was like our son.

Mike was a hard-working person who had all kinds of ideas but in those early years he was a terrible businessman. For example, we had accumulated a mountain of horse manure at the stable. We kept pushing it back and piling it up. Finally, Mike came to me and said, "You know, Doctor, I'd like to go into the business of selling manure. There's a big demand for it, but I'm going to need a truck. I know where there's a good truck and I can buy it cheap." So, I lent him the money to buy the truck, and he planned to make back the money in short order.

He figured he must have had a thousand pickup loads, and at ten dollars a load he could make enough money to pay for his next year in college. I had a tractor with a front-end loader, so he could load the manure onto the truck. He put an ad in the local paper, using my telephone number since he didn't have his own. The phone started ringing off the hook because it was very appealing to get that amount of manure for that price.

I went down to the stable. "Hey, Mike, I said, "thanks a lot for putting my telephone number in your ad. We're going to have

Mike Bruzzi and Joseph D'Alameida, at veterinary school clinic in Italy

to get you a phone here at the stable, because I can't be taking your messages. However, I do have an order for you." So Mike promptly called the man and agreed to deliver a truckload of horse manure to his place.

I saw him down at the stable diligently loading the truck. I had to go out on some calls and when I came home, Mike still wasn't back. By and by, he came driving in with the empty truck. I walked down to the stable to find out how his first real business venture had turned out.

"Well, Mike, you're in business," I said, "you sold your first load of manure."

He said, "Yeah, not exactly."

"What do you mean, not exactly?"

"Well, I delivered this load of manure down in Narragansett. The old man had a beautiful garden with grapevines and toma-toes, just beautiful. I unloaded the manure and piled it for him. He had a wheelbarrow and he showed me where he was going to spread it, so I decided to help him. When I got done, he said he wanted to pay me, and I said, 'Well, let's just forget this one,'" and so, Mike left with no money.

Mike decided to take his next year of school in Italy. He didn't know how to speak Italian, but he learned. We agreed to keep in touch by sending tape recordings back and forth. One day, I was up in the office, and I saw an old truck drive up to our manure pile. I didn't allow people to drive into my stables, so I went back there. The man had backed his truck up to the manure pile. I asked, "Who are you?"

He looked at me, and said, in a heavy Italian accent, "Who are you?"

"Who am I? I own this stable and you're trespassing and I want to know what you are doing here."

"Oh, are you Dr. Kaplan? Well, Mike Bruzzi told me anytime I needed manure, I could just come down here and get it."

"Is that right. Would you like me to get the tractor out and load it for you?"

"Yes. That would be nice."

Needless to say, I told him he would have to load it by pitchfork and the next time to call me and let me know he was coming. Of course, I put that story on a tape to Mike. I enjoyed razzing him about that for years afterwards.

Anyhow, Mike started practicing in Massachusetts and has built up a nice practice. He works seven days a week, from morning till night. I was his mentor. I kept at him and kept at him, so he has a good investment program and paid off his mortgage in three years, the same as I did. When he did, he said, "Well, I beat you." I said, "No. You didn't, but it was pretty much of a tie."

When I think back, what a great source of satisfaction Mike has been to me. In addition to his thriving practice, he is the veterinarian at the Bristol County Agricultural High School in Massachusetts, where he also is a mentor to the students. He has been recognized as Outstanding Practicing Veterinarian in Southeastern Massachusetts.

Little Miss Muffet

Mike Bruzzi started his practice in Massachusetts, just over the line from Rhode Island. Things were very slow at first, and then he was contacted by a wealthy family about taking care of their animals. He became the family's veterinarian and developed a close relationship with them. Their farm encompassed a great deal of land, a beautiful home and new barns, and a variety of animals: sheep, goats, domesticated raccoons, and all kinds of wildlife, every kind of fowl, and a number of horses.

The owners, Leo and Barbara Zuckerberg, were the most unpretentious kind of people you could imagine. Barbara called me at Dr. Bruzzi's suggestion to ask about getting a pony. She said there were a lot of children around, children of friends who visited, and children of the people who worked on the farm. She wanted to be able to provide pony rides for the children. I thought of my client Bonnie Smith, who ran a very nice stable in this area, gave lessons, and took the kids to the horse shows, so I called her. She had just the pony. It was her son David's pony, but he had outgrown her. Bonnie said, "Little Miss Muffet is just like a pet here. She loves children and loves to have them ride her, but she is too small for us now and I think the Zuckerman farm would be an ideal place for her." Arrangements were made and the pony was shipped to Mrs. Zuckerberg, who was thrilled with her. From time to time I would hear about how wonderful this little pony was.

Mrs. Zuckerberg told me a cute story. "You know, that pony now has at least a dozen owners. I want you to know that your friend, Dr. Bruzzi, has given this pony away to at least twelve kids that I know of, and maybe more."

"What do you mean he's given her away?"

According to Mrs. Zuckerberg, Dr. Bruzzi would ask every child he knew who liked horses, and ponies in particular, "How would you like to own a pony? If I give you a pony, you won't have to buy it or take care of it, but it will be your pony."

No little boy or girl could refuse such an offer. He would introduce a child to Mrs. Zuckerberg and tell her, "I just gave this youngster a pony, if it's okay with you." And Mrs. Zuckerberg would play along. The children really believed that they owned the pony and they would tell their friends. They took pictures and made drawings of their pony. Knowing Dr. Bruzzi, I'd say he continued to give Little Miss Muffet away. I imagine that the list has grown to maybe a hundred owners.

My Dog Pip

Richard "Dick" Oster, of Cookson America, owned Lillymere Farm just a few miles north of my house on Route 1. He raised Labrador dogs as a hobby. I was the farm veterinarian and thus became acquainted with the breed and what it took to raise a champion in the field and on the show bench.

Dick had a professional handler, Butch. To get away from the pressure of business he had a cabin built where he delighted in practicing his culinary skills. Many times when I visited the farm the loudspeaker would boom, "Doctor Kaplan, come to the cabin." On one of my visits to the cabin I congratulated Dick and Butch at winning "Best in Show" at a major event. During lunch, Dick asked me if I would like to have a Lab puppy.

One of his best females had just had a litter. We walked to the kennel and he told me to take my pick. They all looked beautiful, so I said, "You guys are the experts." He and Butch looked at each other and they picked up this beautiful black puppy.

I took him home, walked into the house, and as my wife Evalyn greeted me, I said, "Isn't he a pip?"

I had many dogs in my lifetime, the first one when we lived in Kingston, a female Boxer named Sandal. When we bought our land and built the house and hospital, we had Chester, a male Shepherd, and his best friend Peanuts, a red Dachsund. We also had a Springer and a Golden Retriever. They all died of old age.

My younger boy George loved turtles, frogs, baby alligators. They all resided in a spare tub.

We regularly had funerals in the back yard, where we erected monuments. Many clients buried their pets there. Today, there are eight stones made by Buzzi Memorials in Westerly. (Ruth Buzzi is part of that family; she starred in the TVshow *Rowan & Martin's Laugh In*.) I still take care of my little pet cemetery even though all the other pet owners have since died.

Pip was the last dog I had. We spent many happy hours in the woods. There was a large stream that I widened and where I built a pool with a waterfall. I stocked the pool with fish, which the wildlife promptly feasted on. Pip understood every word I said. If he got out of sight, I'd call "Pip," and he would promptly return and sit by my side. I would talk to him: "Didn't I tell you to stay where I can see you?" Then I would reach in my pocket and give him a Pet-Tab vitamin.

Pip moved to Dr. Bruzzi's place at the end of his life, when I couldn't give him the care he needed, exercising him and all.

Pip loved that last year of his life with Dr. Bruzzi, where he lived like a king. He had the run of the hospital. He had a toy animal they called "Lamb Chop" that he carried around everywhere. He was the hospital greeter, and he went to the Post Office and shopping with the technicians. Dr. Bruzzi had convinced me to do the right thing by Pip, and seeing him there for his last year in such luxury gave me great pleasure.

My Kind of People

The Kostarides family were among my favorite clients here. The parents were both high school teachers. Before they had children, they had a little dog named Cutie Pie. The four children came along, but Cutie Pie was still number one in the family. The children were always reminded, "Cutie Pie was here before you were, and you are to treat him with respect." I used to joke that Cutie Pie was almost human. If I believed in reincarnation, I would say that Cutie Pie would have been a wise old person in another life. When Cutie Pie died of old age, he was mourned by the family.

The Kostarides family and pets

At one point later on, they had four dogs: Tiny, a huge Lab-type of dog; Rocky, a beagle they said was retarded but they loved him just the same; Toty, a miniature French Poodle; and Susie. Susie was the oldest of all the dogs. She took medicine for her arthritis and Vasotec, a popular human drug that we use in veterinary medicine, for her heart. Susie was waited on and taken to bed with one of the kids when she was restless at night.

Somebody once told me about running into the Kostarides family at the URI Graduate School of Oceanography at URI's Narragansett Bay Campus, a beautiful site by the water where people can exercise their dogs and enjoy the surroundings. The Kostarides family was there with all four dogs. The three younger dogs were romping and playing, and the wife, Pat, was wheeling Susie in a baby carriage. They wouldn't think of leaving her at home. I said, "Well, you know, that is typical of the family, that's exactly how they treat their animals. That's the way they feel, in a nutshell." These are the kind of people who kept me in practice and keep me interested; it continues to be a great relationship to this day.

Afterword

I want to tell you about my Dad. When I was growing up, I'm sure my childhood was like many others. My Dad told me things and I would think, "What does he know?" Many times I would ignore his advice. And though it is true that he became smarter as I got older, my Dad was not always right (although he thought he was). Like many fathers and sons, we have had our rough spots over the years, but we always found a way to smooth them out. The one thing I always knew was that I was loved and supported. I could count on both my parents in all the ways that are important.

More than the things my Dad told me, it was the example he set, the way he lived his life, that I learned from and remember. My earliest memories are of trips with him to cow and horse farms. This was back in the 1950s when there were many dairy farms and hard-working farmers. My Dad would drive many miles and spend hours treating a cow and charge the farmer such a small sum. Many times he wouldn't even get paid. These farmers were proud men who worked unbelievably hard and had very little to show for their efforts. Even at my young age I realized my father was charging them only what they could afford, which in most cases didn't represent anywhere close to full payment. I remember how he told me how important any one cow was to a farmer, that one good milking cow could be the difference to that farmer's being able to put food on the table.

Many times, my father would be awakened in the middle of the night with an emergency call, and he would leave the house and be gone for hours. He would return tired but would still get up at dawn to make scheduled calls to farms. The only reason my father was able to make a good living was that he had office hours in the evenings for pets. (I used to spend time in the office at night, helping out holding the dogs and cats during treatment.) He used to say it represented twenty percent of his time and eighty percent of his income. In truth it was probably closer to ninety. In all those years I never saw him let a farmer down. He was their lifeline and he was proud of it!

My father is Jewish but not a religious man. But I remember him never charging a member of the clergy, no matter the denomination. This made an impact on me because I knew that, growing up, he had suffered discrimination both in school and life. He could have resented the way he was treated, but instead I don't think I ever heard my father tell a racial or ethnic joke. I think we all have some prejudice in us but I certainly never saw any in my father and I hope that I have not shown any prejudice in my life.

I think in many ways my Dad is a frustrated professor. His greatest joy was taking a young college student who aspired to become a veterinarian and encouraging him in his quest. My Dad would take a student on calls and if the student showed promise, then my father would spend all the time and energy required to get that person into a veterinary school. Since there are so few veterinary schools in this country, sometimes a student would be forced to go overseas. I can remember more than once my Dad provided clothes and money for the trip and always encouragement. Some of these students have become incredibly successful and have never forgotten my Dad.

One of the things my Dad used to say when I was growing up was that friends didn't really matter, that only family mattered. He would say that friends would always disappoint you. This is one case where he was wrong! Some of those students have become his friends and would do anything for him. They owe their many successes to my Dad. In fact I consider him a very lucky man because he has had so many friends. We have both been lucky because we have friends who would do anything for us.

I also remember the innate honesty of my Dad. More than once I remember him returning money to a cashier who had made a mistake. I also remember that when he gave his word, everyone knew that he could be trusted. It was a different time then, but my father made many deals on handshakes and I never saw his word questioned. I have never intentionally lied to anyone in my life and this was because of the importance my Dad placed on honesty.

Many of those things I learned from my Dad were when I was growing up. I still learn things from him to this day. Recently, my Mother suffered from dementia. This is a progressive disease, and she became more and more difficult to handle. He resisted putting her in a nursing home even though it would have made his life much easier. I hope he knows how much I respect and love him for the way he handled this difficult situation.

I hope my father enjoys these sentiments.

JOHN KAPLAN

Editor's Note

As Doc says in his Preface, this book came together with the help of a lot of people. In addition to the people he names, I would like to acknowledge the efforts of the production team, the people behind the scenes who translated Doc's oral history into the book you see today.

- Lynn Hawkins retyped the original 200+ pages on her computer, so that we could share electronic files
- Irene Saxman proofread and copy edited three rounds of revisions
- Maeri Ferguson reviewed the final manuscript before it went for typesetting
- Chris Izzo, of CRI Design, designed the cover and interior, did the page production, and supervised the printing (Chris is also on the board at the Providence Animal Rescue League)
- Casey Conrad donated her imagination and her marketing skills, from working on title and cover ideas, to distribution of the published work
- Help with the photo research includes Jim Hall and Liz Holstein at the Pettaquamscutt Historical Society; Joanne Ricitelli at the South Kingstown Land Trust; Sarina Wyant at the Special Collections Library at the University of Rhode Island; Terri Leifest, Publisher, and Wendy Giordano, editor of "Times Past" at *The Narragansett Times*. Chris Izzo's photos augment the illustrations
- Paul Keane, my brother, and Deborah Coffey, my daughter, lent their critical eyes to the work, . . . and didn't hold back

- Bob and Diane Smith kindly re-read the working manuscript, lending some details of life in South County over several decades

- Ruth Gobeille and Ibby Freeman of the Animal Rescue League of Southern Rhode Island reviewed the original draft and supported me all along with their unbridled enthusiasm

- Most of all, the author himself. It has been a delight to work with Doctor Kaplan. He was always willing to answer my questions and bear with all the details of book production. It's been a great year working together.

When I wanted to see some of the farms where Doc had worked, he drove me around one Sunday, after a hearty breakfast at Friendly's. All the way from the Browning property in Matunuck, to Horseshoe Falls in Shannock, and back home past Jingle Valley Farm in West Kingston, he pointed to the farms and regaled me with his stories.

I hope we have done him justice. He is so deserving of it.

M.J.K.

Mary Keane, editor, and Doc at Casey Farm